Connecting

Return, Revelation, and Revival

The return of Christ, the Bahá'í Revelation,
and Maharishi's revival of the Vedas

by

Robert Mackay

Connecting - Return, Revelation, and
Revival: The return of Christ, the Bahá'í
Revelation, and Maharishi's revival of the Vedas

—

Robert Mackay

The terms Transcendental Meditation®, TM®, TM-Sidhi®, Science
of Creative Intelligence®, Yogic Flying®, Maharishi International
University, MIU, Vedic Science, Maharishi Vedic Science, Global
Country of World Peace, and Amrit Kalash are protected
trademarks and are used under license or with permission.

ISBN 978-1-7781313-1-8 (print)

Every reasonable effort has been made to acknowledge,
and acquire permissions to reproduce, copyrighted
materials used in this text. Please see relevant
Notes, References, and Permissions for details.

For all those who may aspire to something more.

Table of Contents

Preface vii

1. Discovery 1

    Wonder 3

    Paradise 5

    Mission 9

    Return 17

    Stirrings 23

    Confusion 27

    Hope 35

    Initiation 41

    New Horizons 47

    An Auspicious Meeting 53

    MIU 59

    A New Creation 65

    Natural Law and the Vedas 79

    Fully Engaged 87

    Communicating 91

    Moving On 99

2. Reflections 103

    Evaluation 105

        Natural 107

Practical 108

Beneficial 109

Verifiable 110

    Verified through Personal Experience 110

    Verified through Science 111

    Verified through Vedic Tradition 113

Universal 114

Free to Choose 115

Origins 119

The Vedas 119

Revival 120

Divine Teacher 123

Revelation 126

All Knowledge 132

Concealment 134

Harmony 141

Purpose 141

Conflict or Compatible? 145

    The Concept of Suffering 146

    Reincarnation 149

    Fear of God 155

Paths to God 163

Two Aspects of Reality 167

Star Geometry 170

Finding the Lord as God 178

Afterword 185

References 189

Permissions 193

Acknowledgements 195

Preface

I held off writing this book for 35 years. Friends and family advised against it. They were concerned. The time was not right. It might upset people. I figured they had a good point. Or, since the ideas seemed so obvious to me, so important, maybe someone else would write such a book and spare me the effort. But as far as I know, nobody has. Recently, a few changes in my life and in the world suggest that now the time is right. So, although this may be too late for some, or too early for others, I've gone ahead with it.

The purpose is to express how I reconcile my Christian background, my belief in Bahá'u'lláh, and my experience doing the TM® (Transcendental Meditation®) and TM-Sidhi® programs. My heart knows the connections, and my mind feels compelled to explain. I encourage anyone interested in these topics to investigate for themselves and reach their own conclusions. Perhaps this book may assist in some way.

As you read, please understand from the outset that any opinions offered here are my own. These thoughts are based on my personal experience and on what I have learned through the teachings of Jesus, Bahá'u'lláh, 'Abdu'l-Bahá, and Maharishi Mahesh Yogi. Neither Maharishi International University nor the worldwide TM organization (currently known as the Global Country of World Peace), nor any Christian or Bahá'í institution officially endorse these ideas or this book, beyond its direct quotations. All passages from the Bahá'í writings are current translations at the time of this writing. Those few quotes from Maharishi that are not found in published sources are offered as the best of my recollection.

If these quoted scriptures and commentaries, along with my thoughts, help you reach a deeper understanding or bring new ideas to mind, then my object has been attained.

Part 1. Discovery

Part I: Discovery

Wonder

Jesus is back! It must be. But how?

These thoughts came to me as I stood in the entrance of the TM center in Cambridge, Massachusetts. I was looking at a huge golden banner that read, "Maharishi Mahesh Yogi announces the Dawn of the Age of Enlightenment." If this is real, I thought, then Jesus must be back. But how can that be?

I was about to step into something so different, something so totally unlike anything I had ever experienced or even dreamed possible. And yet, somehow, it had to be connected to what I knew, to what I believed in my heart of hearts. Somehow it had to connect.

What brought me here? How did I reach this threshold of opportunity and wonder? And what did I discover? Let me start at the beginning.

Paradise

As far back as I can remember, as far back as I know, God was there. One of my earliest memories of childhood was sitting with my parents and brother in our darkened living room where a single candle was lit. It must have been a home worship service, and we were probably singing hymns or reading from the Bible. As I stared at the candle, my eyes squinting to block out everything else in the room, it came to me that God was there. God was like that candle. He was just there, always there.

God was there for my parents. Mom and Dad met on a blind date arranged by a youth pastor in Kalamazoo, Michigan. They became better acquainted at a Christian summer youth camp in West Virginia, serving underprivileged kids. God was there as Dad proposed to Mom, when they decided that he would attend Union Seminary in New York City to become a Presbyterian minister, to better serve God and humanity.

God was there for their parents, too. He was watching over Mom's mother, descended from a long line of missionaries and preachers stretching back farther than the American Revolution, as she faced tragic losses of several unborn children—until her body was finally able to sustain three successful pregnancies, blessing her with four exuberant daughters. (Mom was a twin.) God was there for her husband, as he struggled with the pain of an army service wound that eventually led to an amputated leg and excruciating agony every day of his life, to a point that no kind of medication or drug could control.

God must have been there for Dad's father as he clung to the back of a streetcar and rode for 18 miles to the outskirts of Detroit to apply for a job driving a milk wagon during the Great Depression. And although I never met her, God was assuredly there for his wife who raised Dad's five cousins when their own mother died at a young age—only to lose two of those precious souls in the Pacific theater of the Second World War, one in a torpedoed, sinking destroyer and the other in the flaming wreckage of a P-38 fighter plane. She never quite recovered from that loss, and passed away too soon. Her devoted service to the poor and destitute in the community during the Great Depression became clear when many of them attended her funeral—dozens of folks that the family had never met.

The example my grandparents set showed us how to live our faith rather than talk about it. There was no Bible thumping among them, no charismatic swoons or tent meetings. Born-again experiences were rarely mentioned. Theirs was more a life of work, service, and of course going to church on Sundays.

And where was God for me? In the background, if I'm being honest. After all, we were living in an earthly paradise. A few months after I was born, Dad graduated from Union Seminary, and accepted "the call" to serve as a campus pastor at Penn State University. We moved into a brand new house built in the middle of an oak forest, in a post-war housing development called Park Forest Village. The front and back yards of every house on the street were filled with oak trees. As it was the peak of the baby boom, most of those houses had lots of kids for my older brother Bill and me to play with. We had lots of toys, plenty of story books that Mom would read to us, and a stack of records with songs that she would play. We even got to watch a half an hour of TV every day. Who could ask for more?

We did learn about God in Sunday school and church. The State College Presbyterian Church where Dad was Associate Pastor was a grand stone structure right downtown. The arched doorways, polished pews, stately pipe organ, and heavy ceiling beams made it feel special. You knew you were safe there, that God was looking over you. We listened to Bible stories and found out about Jesus. But whether at church, Sunday school, or home, what touched me most deeply were the images from hymns and children's songs. God was "Immortal, invisible, God only wise, Thou light inaccessible, hid from our eyes."[1] He could "melt the clouds of sin and sadness, drive the dark of doubt away."[2] I didn't always understand the words, but I got the idea. You might not be able to see God, but He was big and powerful, and could protect you. And He was always keeping an eye on you, as in the song:

Oh, be careful little eyes what you see,
Oh, be careful little eyes what you see,
For the Father up above
   is looking down with love,
Oh, be careful little eyes what you see.[3]

There were other verses for "ears what you hear," and "mouth what you say," and "hands what you do," and more.

Yes, God was there, out there somewhere, watching over even us kids, keeping us safe. And from our side? We had to behave ourselves, and always try to do what was right.

Notes

1. Rev. Walter Chalmers Smith, *The Hymnal*, #66

2. Rev. Henry van Dyke, *The Hymnal*, #5

3. Traditional children's song

Mission

This familiar, comfortable life was destined to change. In the summer of 1961, Dad went to Switzerland for a month-long Student Christian Movement (SCM) seminar. After his return, we seemed to be hosting a lot of foreign students as guests at home. They sometimes made strange food, to Mom's delight, or showed slides of farmers plowing behind oxen in dry fields. It wasn't long before Mom and Dad informed Bill and I that Christ was calling us to serve—in Thailand. We were going on a Mission!

This was a turning point for all of us. Dad's father had recently passed away, and Mom's parents had entered retirement, and were self-sufficient. In addition to her love of adventure and travel, Mom was worried that Bill and I were becoming lost in materialism. She wanted us to know more than the enticing but mediocre life that suburbia was offering.

"Tie-Land?" asked my friends. Or was it "Thay-Land?" Where was that? All I could understand was that it was very far away, on the other side of the world. And we would be gone for longer than I could imagine. It was to be a totally new life. We sold our house and car, and a big North American Van Lines truck came to pack up all our stuff, including two crates of toys.

The first phase was a little closer to home—missionary training for half a year in Stony Point, New York. We joined a couple of dozen families bound for Ethiopia, India, Sarawak and other exotic places. They housed us in newly-constructed dormitories spread over a sprawling campus in a wooded area on the outskirts of town. As our parents studied whatever it was that missionaries need to do, we kids enjoyed all kinds of activities with—and sometimes without—adult supervision. Some evenings Mom and Dad would sit with us in our bedroom for informal worship. Dad taught us a new song, Jesus Calls Us. These verses have stayed with me ever since:

> Jesus calls us o'er the tumult
> > of our lives' wild restless sea
> Day by day His sweet voice soundeth,
> > saying "Christian, follow Me."
> ...
> In our joys and in our sorrows,
> > days of toil and hours of ease
> Still He calls in cares and pleasures,
> > "Christian love Me more than these."[1]

In that summer of 1963, a group of parents, Dad included, left early one morning to travel to Washington DC to march and hear Dr. Martin Luther King speak about racial equality. In the fall we attended school, with split morning/afternoon sessions, due to the large influx of baby-boom kids. Every

The SCC compound had nice gardens, an auditorium, a tennis court, and a few houses where missionary families were living, now including us. Every day Dad would drop Bill and I off at the American-run International School Bangkok (ISB) before he and Mom went to learn Thai—with excruciating effort—at a mission-run language school. After school we'd play with the other American kids on the compound, and on weekends we might go to the movies or the swimming pool at the Royal Bangkok Sports Club. Mom sometimes played tennis there, and Dad occasionally used their golf course. We had a cook named Chenai, and a maid to wash our clothes and clean house. Missionary life didn't seem half bad, eh? Mom got along really well with Chenai, but the only interaction Bill and I had with Thai people were occasional shy conversations with some very kind students.

The real mission lay ahead, in Chiang Mai, a city in the north. A new, government-run university had just opened there, the first of its kind outside of Bangkok. Dad's job was to oversee the construction of a student center like SCC close to the new Chiang Mai University.

Of course, we weren't the first Presbyterian missionaries bound for Chiang Mai. Many had gone before us. They travelled first by elephants, trekking over mountains, through teak forests, and past rice paddies of the small, once-independent kingdoms of Northern Thailand before arriving at this "Jewel of the North." As the decades passed, they arrived by train, then by airplane. On a large tract of land, on the east side of the river, they established a hospital, schools, and other institutions to serve the people of the city itself, and the whole area.

We lived for a couple of years in this epicenter of Christian activity and witness, between the McCormick Hospital across the street and the McGilvary Seminary up the drive, with nursing school dormitories and classrooms on the other side of the compound. Beyond these were the Dara Academy for girls, and the Prince Royal College (PRC) for boys. There was even an English-speaking school for missionary kids: Chiang Mai Coeducational Center (CCC) behind PRC that Bill and I could walk to. Families from various missions lived on our compound and others nearby, and all the kids went to CCC.

After a few more months of agonizing struggle at language school, Mom and Dad called it quits. Dad began work on the student center project, and also started teaching English at the university. Mom picked up her Thai survival skills by shopping at the market every day, much to the dismay of some of the more conservative missionary wives. Since we were living in a foreign country, she went all out in her efforts to adapt. Our Christmas tree the first year was a palm branch spray-painted gold, and then for several years after that a mango branch draped with a fishnet proffering wrapped candies and lit with a green light. "Do you get the symbolism?" she would ask with a twinkle in her eye. "Jesus said, 'I will make you fishers of men.' Get it?" She designed our rattan dining chairs in a "Thai" style, and fell in love with

Thai handicrafts and the people who fashioned them, making frequent visits to the celadon, umbrella, silver smithing and other handicraft villages on the outskirts of town. Yet she also tried to maintain our American identity and lifestyle. She told us that we should never feel that Thailand was our true home, and for better or for worse, I never did. Bill and I and our friends lived in a kind of bubble, doing things that American kids would do—making model airplanes, playing baseball and Monopoly, building forts, and chasing each other around our houses with toy guns. We did everything but watch TV, only because we didn't have one.

Instead, I read books. The school library had over a thousand. I came to know every title, and read every one that was even remotely interesting, from the Hardy Boys to Lord of the Rings. At home we had Tintin books and a few dozen others, but my favorites, the ones I read over and over again, were the Chronicles of Narnia. Although I knew they were just stories, the children, the animals, the places, Aslan the lion, their adventures and the lessons they learned all came alive in my heart.

We went to Sunday school and Thai church every Sunday morning, and American church every Sunday evening before dinner. We also had a brief worship time at school. I loved the songs, but had little interest in the Bible except for the stories and parables of Jesus. Some things seemed so obvious, like the story of the rich young man who asked Jesus how to get to heaven. Jesus told him to just give away all of his money and follow Him. Wow! How easy was that? He was so stupid not to do it. Imagine—he would get to heaven just by giving away his stuff.

But there were other things I didn't understand. Like, why did the teachers and priests argue with Jesus, and why did they and the Romans have Him killed? He didn't do anything wrong. And why did the people shout, "Crucify Him"? On the other hand, why did Jesus let them do it? He was the Son of God, after all. Couldn't He stop them? That part didn't make much sense.

One night, for reasons I don't remember, I sat up for several hours reading the Book of Revelation. It was absolutely terrifying—filled with dragons and beasts and millions of people dying. But I couldn't put it down. I had to know if it ended OK. I can't say that I understood much at all, but I did get the message—if Jesus is ever to come back, be on His side! I made myself a solemn promise that I would join His team if He comes in my lifetime. In fact, for many years, even into adulthood, whenever there was a particularly striking cloud formation, with the sun shining through with golden rays of light, I would ask myself, "Is it now? Is Jesus coming in the clouds?"

As Dad became better acquainted with the university students and faculty, and made progress on the student center, we moved way over to the far side of town, to a house near the airport, on the highway leading to the university, quite close to the land for the new student center. We had to take the city bus to school now, and our friends were all far away. I spent more time reading, and looking forward to going back to the "States".

Notes

1. Cecil Francis Alexander, *The Hymnal*, #223

Return

By the summer of 1968, we had been in Thailand for four and a half years. It was time for our furlough. Every four years or so, Presbyterian missionaries at that time would take a year off to go back to their home country, so that they wouldn't completely lose touch with family or their own culture. Seizing the chance for adventure, Mom and Dad planned the return trip of a lifetime, with stops of several days each in Katmandu, New Delhi, Moscow, Berlin, Innsbruck, Vienna, Turku, Copenhagen, and Rotterdam. Then we sailed on the SS Statendam to New York City. Friends from State College met us at the pier, and the next day drove us to Fir Tree, on Seneca Lake. I felt like I had returned to heaven.

Fir Tree was a magical place for all of us. It was Grandpa's childhood dream. As a poor farmer's son growing up in Rock Stream, New York, he would sometimes walk the mile or two down to Seneca Lake and look with longing at the lake-front mansions of the rich and famous from New York City, enjoying their summers far away from the sweltering urban heat and noise. He promised himself that when he grew up, he would own one of those mansions. After the Great War he worked with Grandma's six brothers, co-founders and owners of the Peelle Company in Brooklyn, building freight elevators and fire doors. As production foreman he earned a decent salary, and the company did well even during the Great Depression. In the 1930's when housing prices collapsed, he seized the opportunity to buy four cottages on Fir Tree Point, the largest of which was actually a hotel for steamboat passengers coming from Watkins Glen and Geneva to Rock Stream. It was a big, two story structure with seven bedrooms, large living and dining rooms, and two huge, full-length porches. His dream came true, in his own lifetime. Grandpa now brought his own family up to the lake from the city to escape the heat. Mom and her sisters spent all their summers at Fir Tree. And they brought their families there every summer as well. As kids, some of our fondest memories were with our cousins at Fir Tree, skipping stones, swimming, sailing, rowing, canoeing, and climbing the cliffs by day. And then sleeping out on the porch with our cousins at night, to the sound of lapping waves on the beach. Now we were back —for a short while.

After a few days at Fir Tree, we returned to New York City where we would live for the next year. Dad used the furlough time to begin a PhD in comparative religion. We lived in an apartment on Claremont Avenue, near the 116th Street and Broadway subway stop. It was just a block away from Union Seminary and Colombia University, where Dad was studying. Bill and I attended the Episcopalian St. Hilda's and St. Hugh's School a few blocks to the south. Right up the street was the Inter-church Center and the Riverside Church, which we attended.

Like Union Seminary, the Riverside Church is a neo-Gothic masterpiece built in the 1920s by John D. Rockefeller, with a cathedral-like sanctuary, stained glass windows, enormous pipe organ, and a 22-story bell tower that we could explore. Just hop on the elevator and ride to the top floor, scale the steel catwalks among the massive bells, and get a fantastic view of the Hudson River and the Palisades of New Jersey to the west, the towers of Manhattan to the south, and the infinite expanse of apartments and office buildings of Brooklyn, Queens, and the Bronx stretching out to the east as far as the eye could see.

Most of the kids at St. Hilda's and St. Hughes School were from upper middle-class families living in various parts of Manhattan who, like our parents, wanted to keep their children out of the notorious public school system. We were taught by nuns, and every Thursday morning there was a worship service with communion led by a priest.

Most of the kids at the Riverside Church were from Harlem. My first brush with black culture came in Sunday school classes, potluck dinners, and my awkward attempts to play basketball in youth group meetings. This was a time when the term "negro" was being replaced by "black", the year that James Forman marched into the Riverside Church, interrupting the worship service to deliver his famous Black Manifesto to demand economic justice and reparations.

The church had a special study program for seventh-graders, a confirmation class to prepare us for confirming our faith in Christ. The content of the course was dry and complicated, but we enjoyed watching strange, avant-garde movies and going on a week-end retreat to a farm Upstate. The goal of the class, the "graduation" as it were, was an enrollment ceremony in which we would become church members. Towards the end of the year we were told that to do so, you could choose to be baptized by immersion, or you could simply confirm your faith by stating, "I believe that Jesus Christ is the Son of God." What? That's it? It was almost too easy. Of course Jesus is the Son of God. Everyone knows that. It's in the Bible. And so I joined the church.

Summer came again, and we flew back to Thailand. Work had progressed on the student center, as the first dormitory was taking shape. The classes at CCC only went up to eighth grade, so Bill went to live in a mission-run youth hostel in Bangkok, and attend ISB. I got very involved in Boy Scouts, attracted to the uniforms, badges, outdoor skills and camaraderie with my friends.

Bill came home on holidays, bringing with him records by strange-sounding rock groups like Blood, Sweat and Tears, Three Dog Night, and Jethro Tull. He would tell stories till late in the night of the antics and mischief that he and the other rebellious missionary kids would get into, much to the annoyance of the conservative Christian house parents. Once he showed me a Danny Orliss book, about a teenager

Friday evening we'd get shots, in preparation for living overseas. One weekend we travelled into New York City for some kind of official business at the Inter-church Center at 475 Riverside Drive. It was a tall, brand new, gleaming office building with heat-sensitive elevator buttons. Just touch them and they light up, and bing! the elevator arrives. This was headquarters for COEMAR, the Commission on Ecumenical Missions and Relations, the big boss. Dad wanted us and everyone else to be very clear that we weren't stuffy old missionaries, we were "Fraternal Workers," working side-by-side with our brethren in Christ.

After a white Christmas at Grandma and Grandpa's house in Rock Stream, New York, we boarded a train for New York City, rode on a jet plane from the newly-renamed JFK airport to Los Angeles where we stayed a couple of days with my cousins and went to Disneyland. Then onwards via Hawaii, Tokyo, and Hong Kong, finally landing in Bangkok in early January to step out on the steaming tarmac at 100 degrees heat and 100% humidity.

The first year in Bangkok meant more preparation for Mom and Dad. We stayed at the Student Christian Center (SCC), a walled compound in the heart of the city, with a large dormitory for Christian students, men and women, who were studying at the nearby Bangkok Christian College, and possibly other locations as well. We were there to get "acclimated" to life in Thailand, and see how a student center operated.

attempting to live a Christian life in a secular world. It condemned rock music as the "devil's diversion," which we thought was pretty laughable. But Danny or one of his Christian friends said something that I couldn't quite grasp: "You need to do more than go to church to be a real Christian." What did that mean? What is a real Christian?, I wondered. The book didn't seem to offer a direct answer, at least not one that I could understand.

By the next summer, Dad's mission was nearing completion. It looked like he could wrap things up in one more year. Unlike most missionaries who stay on indefinitely, Dad pushed to have a Thai administrator run the student center, and he would then bow out. At the same time, he and Mom were getting concerned about the situation in the youth hostel in Bangkok. They didn't agree with the theological or disciplinary approach of the house parents. So they decided that Bill and I should return to the States a year early, while they would spend their final year living in a student room in the newly-completed dormitory of the student center. Bill was reluctant to leave, but I was overjoyed with the plan. I was far less attached to Thailand than he was, and longed to be "back home", in the States, and return to real life. The arrangement was that Bill would spend the year with Grandma and Grandpa in Rock Stream, and I would go to Stony Brook.

Stirrings

The Stony Brook School is a private Christian school located in Stony Brook, Long Island, near New York City. At that time, my Uncle Donn, the husband of Mom's sister, Aunt Norma, was headmaster. He was the son of Frank E. Gaebelein, founding headmaster of the school and editorial consultant for the New Schofield Reference Bible.

Dad and Uncle Donn had an interesting relationship. Mom and her sisters all got married around the same time, and their husbands came from different political and religious backgrounds. Dad and Uncle Donn were both strong and vocal Democrats, while Grandma, Grandpa, and the two other brothers-in-law were Republicans. On the other hand, Uncle Donn and Aunt Norma were conservative, born-again Christians, while Mom and Dad were very liberal in their beliefs. I've been told that before I was born the political and religious discussions got quite heated. They rapidly turned into arguments that got so bitter that finally one day Grandpa said, "ENOUGH!" and permanently banned all talk of religion or politics in any family gathering.

I was aware of little of this at the time, and got along fine with Aunt Norma, Uncle Donn, and my cousins. I was just glad to be back in America where there was fall, winter, and spring, where I could eat the food, read the signs, and talk to everyone. I lived in a dorm with a roommate, made new friends, listened to records, built model airplanes, and did OK in class. For the longer holidays I travelled to Rock Stream to spend time with Bill, Grandma and Grandpa.

Coming back from one such visit over March spring break, I took a bus from Elmira as always to New York City. Then, before boarding the train to Stony Brook, I saw a book at a newsstand: *Catcher in the Rye*. I remembered seeing Mom reading that book, and so bought a copy. Here I was, a kid taking a train from New York City to a private boarding school reading a book about a kid leaving a private boarding school by train to New York City. I felt completely in his shoes. Although I couldn't understand why Holden Caulfield was so unhappy, I did pick up on the rebel spirit. When I got to Stony Brook it was a day early. Nobody was around, so I went to my room and finished reading the book.

The next day was my 15th birthday. I walked through the empty campus and paused on the sidewalk between Hegeman Chapel and Gaebelein Hall. It dawned on me at that moment, on that bleak, gray, mid-March day that I needed to stop worrying so much about toys, games, and model airplanes, and think more about the important things in life. My glorious vision of life in America had been dimming in the past couple of years, and this was a turning point. Suddenly the allures of consumer life paled against the threat of nuclear war that I had felt since childhood, the evils of the Vietnam War that got worse every year, and the looming fear of communism behind both. Added to these were pollution, racism, poverty, drug addiction and crime. In short, this country that I had so looked forward to returning to, this "home" of mine, was a mess. The song on my King Crimson album summed it up well —my epitaph would simply be "Confusion."

Later that spring there was a special worship service in Hegeman Chapel, led by a dynamic, evangelical preacher. He gave a passionate talk, and then invited anyone who wanted to give their life to Christ to stand and come forward. I was not familiar with this kind of invitation, coming right in the middle of a church service. Of course I wanted to give my life to Christ. I stood up and went forward. It was wonderful. It all made sense. Why not give your life to Jesus? After all, he's the Son of God. Follow Him and all will be well. Returning to my seat, I felt great. Walking out of the chapel into the beautiful sunshine and flowering forsythia bushes was heavenly. But nothing else happened after that, and life continued.

Around that same time, we had been reading *A Tale of Two Cities* in English class. One Saturday morning we had a special session at Gaebelein Hall to celebrate finishing the book by watching a movie about it. Near the end of the movie Sydney Carton takes the place of Charles Darnay to save him from the guillotine. In the cart on the way to his execution he meets another prisoner, a young woman, and there is a very intimate sharing between them as he tries to calm her fears. During the last few moments of the film, when the two of them were exchanging final words, I felt deeply emotional, my heart filling with an indescribable mixture of love, longing, and sadness. Things came to an abrupt end as the guillotine blade came down, and all went black. When we got up to go, I had a strange sensation of being completely independent of my body. I felt my feet walking, my hands moving, and heard my voice talking to my friends, but I, the reality of me, was totally independent and separate. It was almost as if my body was like a car, and I was driving it. This was not an out-of-body experience. I was completely associated with my body, yet at the same time completely independent of it. The sensation continued as we left the building and walked up the street to the dining hall. It lasted through most of lunch, gradually fading. And then life continued.

Confusion

For the next few years I felt strangely lost in a familiar world. Mom and Dad returned to the USA, and we were based in Rock Stream with Grandma and Grandpa for a year. Dad lived in New York City, continuing work on his PhD, and commuting back home every other weekend. Bill spent most of his time with his friends. He grew disillusioned with God to the point that he pretty much quit the church. The next year he went off to Boston University, while Mom, Dad, and I moved back to the State College area. There I finished high school with some of the same classmates as I had in first grade. But things were different now. I didn't fit. The joy was gone.

By this time I had lived in ten houses, attended eight schools, and made and lost seven sets of friends. I began thinking, "Why should I make new friends here when we'll be leaving at the end of the year?" I grew my hair long and hung out sometimes with the derelicts in the pool hall and pinball parlors, and sometimes with the geeks and intellectuals who played bridge at lunch time and carried around stacks of computer punch-cards. I listened to mysterious ballads by the Moody Blues that let my mind roam, and mournful plaints by the Bee Gees to cheer myself up. After all, no matter how bad I felt, the guys who couldn't tell a joke without making everyone cry had to be in even worse shape.

Mom, Dad, and I joined the Diakonia Church that met in the homes of its well-intentioned members to avoid the cost of a building, allowing us to donate more money to worthy causes. But the church seemed less and less relevant to my life. When a youth leader asked what we each believed in, I replied "logic", to which he had no response. Once we went on a family retreat to a hunting lodge, and had a Sunday morning guided group meditation where we all sat in a circle and held hands. Afterwards people raved about how meaningful the experience had been, but my mind had simply wandered, as it usually did whenever they said prayers in church. So much for meditation, I thought.

My hopes and dreams during those years were on boats and sailing. Uncle Jim, one of Mom's cousins, had a cottage at Fir Tree, and he had boats—a 30-foot Chris Craft, a Rhodes 19 sailboat, a 20-foot Penn Yan runabout for water-skiing, and more—all of which he hired me to maintain and operate. Then he started a business selling Hobie Cats, catamaran sailboats from California, and that became the main focus. All summer every summer I lived in the big cottage and spent every waking hour with Uncle Jim assembling, demonstrating, sailing, selling, and delivering Hobie Cats. He started sailboat races on Seneca Lake every Sunday, and the Hobie Cats always won, and so people started buying them. I was absolutely gung-ho, and won more than my fair share of races.

Somehow sailing gave me a glimpse of perfection. There was beauty in the water, the waves, and the clouds, the shape of the boat's hull and the curve of the sails. There was science in weather prediction, in the physics of hydrodynamics, air flow, resistance, and lift. There was the art of navigating within a two-dimensional moving matrix of racing boats, and the intuitive feel of the helm on an upwind beat to optimize boat speed. It was a harmony of man, nature, and technology.

Winning races against adults gave me confidence. I began challenging myself, demanding more. All through primary school teachers commented that I did not apply myself. School was easy, and I was content to coast along, getting As and Bs, with the occasional C in handwriting. In 12th grade, for the first time ever, I really applied myself to my studies, took some Advanced Placement classes, and wound up getting straight As in all subjects but gym class. I found and treasured the passage in the Bible, at the end of the Beatitudes, where Jesus said, "You, therefore, must be perfect, as your heavenly Father is perfect."[1] And didn't Jesus say to the lame man that he healed, "See, you are well! Sin no more, that nothing worse befall you."[2] I knew that Jesus had died for my sins, and that I was forgiven. But that was not enough. I was tired of sinning. I wanted to "sin no more." I wanted to become perfect.

I sometimes challenged Dad, asking him how I could be absolutely certain I would go to heaven. "Well," he would reply, "we can't ever be sure..." He did not offer the standard "born-again" response. In fact, he often said that he didn't see how the born again experience was necessary, since he himself had never had one. And when it came to Christianity solving the problems of the world, he also had doubts. He used to ruefully quote a prominent theologian and critical thinker who said that Christianity is busy rearranging deck chairs on the Titanic.

When it came time to go to university, I chose Penn State because it was familiar and inexpensive. Finally, I thought, I'll be getting some answers. Now I will find out what all of those students that Dad used to work with were learning. My favorite subject in high school had been geometry, because it was clean, logical, and flawless. So I started on a B.A. in Mathematics. I was accepted into a dorm in North Halls, where they offered co-ed living according to interest groups. I went for the Individual in a Complex Society group, hoping to meet others who also could not figure out the world or their place in it. I never bothered to attend church while living in the dorm.

I had no idea what I might actually do with a degree in math, since the only career options were actuary or computer scientist. But since it was a B.A., I could take all kinds of liberal arts courses like Philosophy, Art History, Psychology, and Life in Ancient Greece. Now it was time to get some answers. Unfortunately, the answers didn't come. The philosophy professor introduced, built up, and then shattered each philosopher in turn, like ducks in a shooting gallery. The psychology professor was a hard-core behaviorist who was fixated on Pavlov's dogs. He used a standard deviation curve to determine our grades, as in 13% get As, 34% get Bs, 34% Cs, 13% Ds, and the rest fail. The math classes were also disappointing, as I struggled with calculus. I could work through the equations OK, but could not get an intuitive grasp on functions, limits, or infinity. I was just pushing numbers and symbols around on the page.

Most of my friends in the dorm were engineering students from blue-collar families of Pittsburgh and Philadelphia who just wanted to gut this out to get a good job. They studied hard and weren't interested in asking questions. However, I was lucky enough to have a roommate for a few months who was different. Gus and I had long conversations about things we thought were important. Late one night, out on the golf course, staring up at the stars, he told me, "Bob, you are on a search." Wow. So I was on a search. I had never thought about it that way.

I was getting few answers, though. The rebel side of me couldn't see the sense of studying things you hate just to get a good job, get married, and have a house in the suburbs with a wife and kids. It all seemed so pointless. And yet, I now started wondering whether my rejection of the status quo and lifestyle made sense. Maybe I was wrong and everyone else was right. All through high school and my first year at Penn State I had refused to drink beer or alcohol at all, or to try pot. All my friends did, but I doubted my ability to control myself, and I didn't think it would be good for me. Now I wasn't so sure. Everyone I knew except Grandma and Grandpa drank, at least a little sometimes. So I began drinking occasionally and smoked a little pot. But still no significant answers came.

Back home, Dad was called to serve as pastor for the Upper Spruce Creek Presbyterian Church, still near State College. Mom and Dad moved into the manse, and began ten years of service to the sincere, hard-working folks of the valley. I transferred my church membership, and attended church and Sunday school whenever I was home, but my life was at Penn State now.

I joined the sailing team, and started driving the campus bus. Soon I was driving the bus more hours than I spent in class or doing homework combined. My grades started slipping. From the middle of the first year, I had been telling Dad that I wasn't really getting much out of college. I just didn't see myself fitting in with whatever it was supposed to be preparing me for. "Stick it out," he would say, "Just stick it out."

In the spring of my second year I read a book, *The Case Against College* that challenged many common assumptions, and resonated with my intuitions about life. I went over to the Guidance Center where they had a large board on the wall with dozens of careers you could get with a Penn State degree. I went through the entire list, and not one job appealed to me. So I decided to leave.

The plan was to take a year off, share an apartment with my friend, Barry, earn some money driving a milk truck, and then maybe go to a Penn State branch campus and major in graphic design. After final exams, eight of us on the sailing team spent a weekend sailing around the Chesapeake Bay, walking the streets of Annapolis, eating crabs, drinking beer, and telling stories long into the night as we lay at anchor in secluded bays. Once we saw a small Coast Guard boat working on buoys, and my friend Sue told me about Cape May, where there is a big Coast Guard base and training facility.

When I got home, I called the milk company to see when I could start, and they told me there was no job. Sitting there in Dad's study in the manse, I started thinking, "What do I really want to do with my life?" The answer was not long in coming: "What I really want to do is join the Coast Guard!"

Notes

1. *The Bible*, Revised Standard Version, Matthew 5:48
2. Ibid, John 5:14

Hope

Dad was not at all pleased with the idea of me joining the military. He had served in the U.S. Army during WWII and hated it. The war itself was not the issue. He was in the Engineering Corps towards the end of the war, and spent most of his time blowing things up and building Bailey Bridges for the advance of troops through Germany. What he hated was the army itself, the stupidity, bureaucracy, and mediocre mentality. He feared that I would encounter the same in the Coast Guard. I only saw the snazzy uniforms, exotic duty posts, and cool missions like search and rescue, lighthouse keeper, and arctic exploration. It was just like the Boy Scouts, but with boats—and you get paid! From the recruiter I got a poster of a 44 foot motor lifeboat crashing through the waves, with the message boldly printed across the bottom, "The Coast Guard - It's not just a job, it's an adventure!"

That fall I went to Cape May for boot camp, and by January of 1977 was serving at Coast Guard Station Gloucester, MA as a Seaman Apprentice. The station had a 44 foot motor lifeboat just like in my poster, along with a 41 foot utility boat and a Boston Whaler skiff. Duty consisted of shifts in the comm room working the radio and teletype, and an occasional "boat job" where we would head out into rough seas to find and tow in broken-down fishing boats. The Gloucester fishing fleet was in marginal repair, and things always seemed to go wrong in the worst weather.

We worked port and starboard shifts, meaning 5 days on duty with 2 days off one week, followed by 2 days on duty and 5 days off the next. So we had lots of free time, but not much to do, particularly for the single guys like me. Bill had finished his degree in Boston University, and was living in Cambridge. Often on long weekends I would take the train to Boston and stay with him and his roommates. Otherwise, on days off, I would kill time by walking around Gloucester. I tried attending church once, but nobody even said hello. One day that spring I wandered into the town library and saw a book, *The TM Program ... What It Is, How It Works, What It Does* by Philip Goldberg. I got curious. One of my roommates at Penn State had been involved in this TM thing a little. So I decided to check it out.

"The Transcendental Meditation® Program is a proven approach to developing full human potential"[1] the title page said. According to the book, people have it all wrong about life. We were not born to suffer, we were born to be happy. "Life is here to enjoy,"[2] it quoted Maharishi Mahesh Yogi, the founder of the TM program. TM, the book said, "enables every individual to harness and cultivate creative intelligence, or consciousness, in his or her life. Natural and simple, based on the natural working of the mind, the technique provides, in the short run, rejuvenation to the mind and body, greater energy, clarity of thinking, efficiency in action, tranquility, and other proven benefits that are widely known. In the long run it is the key to fulfillment, enlightenment, and the restoration of human dignity."[3]

Wow. I was amazed. The book spoke directly to my frustrations and questions in a calm, logical, and reassuring way. I could not find a single loophole anywhere. It described the benefits of a simple, natural, effortless technique that could be done almost anywhere by anyone. Just sit for 20 minutes with your eyes closed twice a day, and you will transform yourself and society. There was a scientific chart that displayed significant drops in metabolic rates, illustrations of restful alertness in brain wave activity, and a diagram showing how the mind settles down from a turbulent state of thinking to finer and finer levels of thought, until it reaches pure consciousness, a boundless state of perfect order and stability.

How it works, said the book, is by allowing the mind to experience pure consciousness. You couldn't learn how to do it from this book, or from any book. You learn through a systematic, seven-step process led by a TM teacher who provides a mantra and teaches you how to use it. The mantra is a sound, which when used as instructed, allows the mind to experience finer and finer levels of thought in a natural and effortless way, until it reaches the source of thought, or pure consciousness, where the mind is simply aware of itself.

It's as if you are in a theater, the book explained, watching a movie. The projectionist starts to blur the picture to the point that it fades out altogether, and you only see the silver screen. That's like the mind experiencing itself, with no thoughts. The word "Transcend" in Transcendental Meditation refers to the natural ability of the mind to go beyond superficial thoughts and experience pure consciousness. Scientists identified unique physiological and brainwave characteristics showing how the mind is in a state totally different from sleeping, dreaming, or waking state. They postulated a 4th state of consciousness, and called it Transcendental Consciousness, or TC for short. It is a state of restful alertness.

This experience of TC, or pure consciousness, has an effect on daily life. The deep rest gained while doing TM allows the body to throw off stress. From the very first day you learn, the book said, you will begin to notice the effects. Although everyone is different, it mentioned preliminary scientific studies showing changes and improvements in body, mind, behavior, and personality. The list was quite long, including decreased anxiety, increased creativity, faster reaction times, greater emotional stability, more agility, faster learning, better job performance, decreased irritability and many more. The idea is that by enlivening the experience of pure consciousness, all aspects of your life improve. It's similar to how watering the root of a tree gives life to the whole tree—every leaf, branch, and fruit.

"When, during the Transcendental Meditation technique," the book quotes Maharishi, "the mind transcends the subtlest state of thought and attains the state of Self-consciousness, or pure Being, it attains the level of cosmic law. Coming out of that state, its position is like that of a man entering the office of the President and coming out endowed with his goodwill."[4]

The "state of Self-consciousness" or "pure Being" are other terms that refer to pure consciousness or Transcendental Consciousness (TC). Another term sometimes used is the pure field of creative intelligence, which is the home of natural law. As you continue to meditate, your nervous system becomes accustomed to the experience of TC, to the point where it begins to infuse your waking, dreaming, and sleeping states. Reading that I was reminded of what I experienced back at Stony Brook after the *Tale of Two Cities* movie. Was this the same thing? When you experience TC all the time, the book continued, that is called cosmic consciousness, or CC. "The person in cosmic consciousness has a permanent mandate," explains Goldberg. "All the laws of nature support his actions."[5] Thus, when you are in CC you live in accord with all of the laws of nature.

This sounded too good to be true. Would living in accord with all the laws of nature be the same as a life free from sin? Could that be possible? But there was more.

Maharishi was thinking big. He had a World Plan. Developing the full potential of the individual person would improve government achievements, realize the highest ideals of education, eliminate crime and unhappiness, optimize use of the environment, fulfill economic aspirations, and achieve the spiritual goals of mankind.

That all sounded pretty grand. My feeling was that if this can just help me be a better person in so many ways, that would be fine. Maybe it could help me become a better Christian. I wasn't sure if it was possible to live a life free of sin, but I sure wanted to. I hadn't heard this idea even mentioned before. Maharishi was offering enlightenment. That's what I wanted. I wanted to be enlightened.

Until I read that book I had rarely said a prayer, but upon finishing it I prayed to God not to let me die before I learned TM.

Notes

1. Philip Goldberg, *The TM Program*, title page

2. Maharishi Mahesh Yogi, quoted in *The TM Program*, p 10

3. Philip Goldberg, *The TM Program*, p 17

4. Maharishi Mahesh Yogi, quoted in *The TM Program*, p 127

5. Ibid, p 127

Initiation

Of course, there was part of me that was skeptical. I had been let down so many times in the past, and had grown cynical. The book had said that to get the best results you had to be regular, and meditate every day, in the morning after you get up and in the evening, ideally before dinner. So I decided, that to give it a fair test, I would try to do that, and meditate as regularly as possible. I would keep an open mind for six months, and then I would decide if it was OK for me.

Then there was the issue of the course fee. It wasn't cheap. They had a sliding rate scale, and being a fully employed adult, I was at the top. It would cost me more than 1/3 of my monthly salary. But then I started doing some calculations, and figured out that if I meditated for a year or two, each meditation would cost me less than a can of pop. The longer I meditated, the cheaper it would get. And besides, they said they'd check my meditation as often as I wanted, for free. Not a bad deal.

I got permission from our chief petty officer for four consecutive days off duty for a "self-improvement" program, and headed to Boston to stay with Bill. Walking into the Cambridge TM center, I saw the sign, "Maharishi Mahesh Yogi announces the Dawn of the Age of Enlightenment." At that moment a small voice in my mind said: "Jesus is back!" I didn't spend much time pondering the implications and possible contradictions at that point, though. I was determined to move ahead.

The date of my instruction was May 29th, 1977. From that day onwards, my life has never been the same. The experience of meditation itself was fine, pretty much as expected, as far as I could tell. It was as easy as the book had said it would be. My teacher, Vicki, was very positive and supportive. What enthralled me was how I felt during the rest of the day, and the days that followed. It was like walking in a cloud of bliss, but at the same time completely connected and aware. My heart was singing and I couldn't stop smiling. Everything was fine, just fine. It was as though a huge ball of fear and stress that I had been holding onto so tightly simply melted and slipped through my fingers. The joy was back.

By the end of the week that initial sublime feeling faded, or maybe I became accustomed to it. In any case, it never went completely away. Each day, no matter how stressed out I became, my daily miracle, TM, restored that feeling to some degree.

My first challenge was to incorporate TM into my life in the Coast Guard station. I decided to keep it a secret, so that the other guys wouldn't make fun of me, or disturb me, or even prevent me from meditating. Every morning I'd get up 1/2 hour early, enter the unheated stairwell of our modern, 3-story station, and take the stairs up to the top landing that accessed the roof. There I would meditate, and in the afternoons, before dinner, the same. I was always a bit fearful that someone would climb that last flight of stairs for some reason and discover me, but they never did. Each time, coming back down those stairs, I felt refreshed and energized, my mind clear, and my soul at peace.

As the months went by, I noticed changes in my moods and behavior. I got angry less frequently, and became more optimistic. I didn't seem to get colds as often, and quit biting my fingernails. I could think more clearly. I stopped smoking pot, and went out drinking less. I quickly discovered that drinking made me feel worse, not better, than meditating. I advanced through the ranks, and became a 3rd Class Petty Officer—a Boatswain's Mate, and soon earned my Coxswain's pin. That meant I was qualified to run the boats, and I had my own crew. We towed in more fishing boats in routine boat jobs, and had some harrowing moments as well. Through it all, I had a secret, an edge, a kind of quiet but special superpower that kept me calm in the face of stress and storms, and always a bit on the cheerful side. The six-month mark that I had set for making a decision came and went unnoticed. The value of TM was self-evident.

Outside of the Coast Guard station, word got around. Bill knew, of course, and I used to share with him and his roommates how cool this was. I told Mom and Dad, and by the time I showed up at Fir Tree that summer the whole family knew. Nobody said anything, but reading between the lines I could tell that some were not happy. Aunt Norma and

Aunt Mary were strong born-again Christians, and although they never spoke to me about TM, they warned Mom that I was dealing with the devil and was bound straight for hell by following this cult. Mom stood up for me, saying that she was seeing positive changes in my life, and so it must be good. Aunt Grace, Dad's sister, shared her concerns that I was involved with a cult, but Dad reassured her that he did not think it was.

Although unaware of these conversations, I knew the feeling. In fact, similar questions came to my mind, but in a different way. On the one hand, I knew that this was good. It was very good. It was better than anything I had heard of, read about, or experienced. I decided that since it was so good, it must be from God. But exactly how, I did not know. I didn't know much about it, but it seemed like it could unravel the problems of philosophy and psychology. It was so simple, and yet so profound. It felt right, all the way to the core.

On the other hand, there was no trace or suggestion of TM in the Bible or in what I understood from my Christian upbringing. Jesus certainly never spoke of it, and He never instructed anyone in meditation, that I knew of—at least, not like this. Maharishi was from India, and probably a Hindu.

I found out that there was a TM center near Gloucester, just down the coast in Beverly Farms. I went there to have my meditation checked. This was a free service for anyone who learned to meditate, just to make sure that you are still meditating correctly. There they told me about advanced lectures and residence courses, which sounded interesting.

Residence courses were weekend group retreats where you did extra meditation sessions under the guidance of TM teachers, and learned more about TM and the philosophy behind it. A couple of times that winter they booked vacant guest houses in Gloucester, and 10 or 12 of us would spend the weekend. They taught us simple yoga postures called "asanas", and a breathing exercise called "pranayam". These were two parts of a "round", which consisted of asanas, pranayam, meditate, and rest that took about an hour. Instead of single, 20-minute meditations, we did two rounds in the morning and two more rounds in the evening during the weekend. They told us that this gave more rest to our bodies, which would allow deeper experiences.

In the advanced lectures and residence courses we heard audio tapes and watched video tapes of Maharishi giving talks. He spoke a lot about the experience of pure consciousness, which was nice, but it didn't have much meaning for me. I told the TM teachers that I was not having the kinds of experiences during meditation that he described. That will come, they told me. The fact that I was getting the benefits showed it was working.

New Horizons

In the summer of 1978 I was transferred to Coast Guard Cutter Northwind, a polar icebreaker homeported in Wilmington, North Carolina. My dream job just kept getting better. Over the next few years we travelled to Point Barrow on the north slopes of Alaska, to McMurdo Sound in Antarctica, to the Sondestrom Fiord in Greenland, and to numerous islands, countries, and ports of call in between, on missions to support scientific research, military activities, and ice-breaking operations.

When I first arrived on board, I saw this as a fresh start. Among other things it was an opportunity to stop drinking completely, simply by telling everyone from the outset that I didn't drink or smoke pot. Finding a place to meditate was a bigger challenge. The ship had a few out-of-the-way compartments, but you never knew when someone was going to come walking through. The only private space was my bunk, but it wasn't that private. There were about 60 of us, seamen and junior petty officers, sleeping in a cramped berthing area, with bunks stacked 3 high. Eventually I figured out a way to rig some curtains around my bunk, and poking my head up between beams and pipes, was able to sit up to meditate. Life was bliss.

Meditating on a ship was challenging in another way. You are supposed to sit comfortably, and that's fine when the ship is in port, tied up at the pier. Underway is another story, especially on an icebreaker like ours, which had no keel; instead below the waterline it was shaped like half a football sliced lengthwise. In the open water it was constantly rolling, and when we were breaking ice the sound and movement were like an earthquake in a hailstorm. But usually it was not so bad. I was able to adapt, and rarely missed a meditation.

The Northwind was getting old, and in need of serious repair. After the first summer in the Arctic, we spent a full year in port, preparing for our next deployment to Antarctica. The ship was moored at the municipal pier in downtown Wilmington, and we got to know the town, with its tree-lined streets, parks, and nearby beaches very well. The people were friendly, and the weather was warm. One Sunday in spring I put on my dress uniform and gathered up the courage to go to the Presbyterian Church. I was welcomed with open arms.

For the first time ever in church, I felt that I understood what it was all about. A veil had lifted. Based on my experience doing TM, things now made sense. The Bible verses seemed to be describing pure consciousness. The sermon corresponded with some of Maharishi's talks. The words in the hymns came alive, and I was moved to tears as I sang out with reverence and gusto. So this was what it was all about. Looking around me, though, it seemed that nobody else was "getting it." They were going through the motions, but their faces told me that

The Bahá'í Faith was certainly appealing. In a goodbye conversation with Mary before I left for MIU, I surprised myself by saying, "I could never become a Bahá'í. What would my father say?" She just nodded. At that moment it dawned on me that I was considering the possibility.

A few weeks later, back in Pennsylvania, I found myself asking Dad, "What would you think if I became a Bahá'í?"

"Well," he said slowly, "I don't know..." and the talk shifted to other topics.

I was left to ponder the very little that I knew of Jesus, Maharishi, and Bahá'u'lláh. Each of these three seemed so different, so unapproachable, so beyond my comprehension. And yet each seemed to play an important role in the world, or at least in my life. Could there be any connection between them?

they didn't see what I was seeing. How could I tell them? I enthusiastically greeted and thanked the minister on the way out the door, fairly certain by this time that I may have gained more from his words than he had intended to put into them. How could I tell him? In any case, I went back often, and always felt at home.

This new-found enthusiasm and love for life spilled out in other ways. Some of my shipmates played guitar, and they helped me learn. I had never had the confidence or manual dexterity before, but now I was able to overcome my fears and fumbling fingers. I got a book to teach myself how to type, and spent hours in a nearby trade school hammering away until I gained a decent level of proficiency. I read a book, *Food is Your Best Medicine* by Dr. Henry Beiler, got interested in diet and exercise, and started eating more healthy foods. Several evenings a week I would run over to the Greenfield Lake Park, around the whole lake and back, about 5 miles in total. Back in high school I could barely run a block. And I got a 10-speed bike that I would ride all over town. I joined an environmental group, Harmony with All Living Things, and attended meetings and protests.

There was no TM center in Wilmington, but I did get to know a local TM teacher, Rosemary, and her boyfriend, Tom. One weekend the three of us drove up to Chapel Hill for a TM residence course, with me crammed into the luggage space of their little VW Karmann Ghia. The course went well, and on the way back Rosemary told me that Maharishi had started a university where everyone meditates. It was called Maharishi International University, or MIU for short.

The next day I went to Fir Tree for a week, and had one of the best times ever with my cousins, aunts, and uncles. For the return trip to North Carolina, Uncle Donn and Aunt Norma were driving to Washington DC, and gave me a ride that far. For the entire 6-hour journey, Aunt Norma slept in the back seat while Uncle Donn talked non-stop about the value of education, and that I should go back to college. By the time we got to Washington, I was convinced.

I got more information from Rosemary about MIU. Maybe there I could learn to become a TM teacher. By this time I knew that TM was the best thing in the world. It had helped me so much, and I wanted to share it with everyone. I had originally joined the Coast Guard with a plan to either become a tugboat captain, or to gain the money and skills necessary to sail around the world. But those were just dreams. And my appetite for seafaring had been satisfied by our various journeys.

Being a TM teacher seemed like a much better calling. And there was more. Maharishi was talking about a World Government of the Age of Enlightenment. TM teachers would be "Governors" in this system. There were ministries of education, health, agriculture, business, and others. Maybe I could get involved in that. Or maybe I could find out more about where TM comes from, and if it's from God. In fact, the whole thing felt a little like the Kingdom of God on earth that Jesus would establish when He returned. Could that be possible? Probably not, but if it was, I certainly wanted to be in on it. This was what I wanted to do with my life.

So I wrote to MIU asking if they had some sort of major where I could become a TM teacher. They sent me a beautiful catalog all about Education for Enlightenment. It looked like a dream come true. The letter said no, they didn't offer TM teacher training, but come anyway. And so I did.

My enlistment finished in October 1980, too late for the fall semester, but I could start in January, they said. I spent a month with Grandma and Grandpa in Rock Stream, and a few weeks with Bill in Massachusetts. Then back to Pennsylvania with Mom and Dad for Christmas before heading off to MIU.

An Auspicious Meeting

Now I need to backtrack a bit to include an important part of the story. Back in the fall of 1977 Bill moved from Cambridge to Amherst to work on an MS in Geology at the University of Massachusetts, or UMass. Instead of the train, I now had to catch a ride with my buddies travelling home from Gloucester for the weekend, and hitchhike the rest of the way for a visit. Bill lived in a small house in town with three roommates. I would still go into Boston occasionally to visit Barry, my friend from Penn State, who had moved there and was living in Brookline at that time.

One Sunday evening, after a dinner of burgers and beer, it was time for Barry to head home, and me to return to the Coast Guard station. We rode back towards Barry's apartment on the Green Line, a trolley that runs along Commonwealth Ave. At one stop I noticed a girl about my age get on. There was something different about her, something that I somehow recognized. "Now she looks like the daughter of a missionary," I remember thinking. Our eyes met. She moved up into the car and stood near us. I continued talking with Barry until he got off at his stop.

"Do you know how to get to North Station?" the girl then asked.

"Sure," I replied, "I'm going there myself. I'll show you."

We walked together from the trolley stop to North Station through a maze of tunnels and ramps, finally arriving at the ticket booth. She bought a ticket for Ipswich, meaning that we'd be taking the same train up the coast as far as Beverly, where she would transfer.

Her name was Mary. She was a student at UMass, and was going to Ipswich to visit her grandfather. She had grown up in Nicaragua, and her parents and siblings were still living there. They were Bahá'í pioneers. The Bahá'í Faith was a new religion, she told me. I had certainly never heard of it. They believed in God, that all religions are from God, and that all of us are children of God. The purpose of the religion was unity, to unite humanity. They had a new Prophet, named "Bahá'u'lláh," which means the "Glory of God." Pioneers were like missionaries, people who move to other places to help teach the Bahá'í Faith. I told her about growing up in Thailand in a missionary family, and we marvelled at the serendipity of this chance encounter.

Since she was studying at UMass, I asked if I could look her up the next time I went out to visit Bill, and she agreed. She was staying with a family, Nat and Carol and their two children, in a big house in the woods outside town. Nat was a professor of media at UMass, and they would sometimes have evening meetings at their house, called "firesides," that Mary would invite me to. I learned a little more about the Bahá'í Faith there, and it all sounded fine to me. Most of the things they were saying, like elimination of prejudice, equality of men and women, harmony of science and religion, were all things that I believed in. Everyone was so friendly, and it seemed that no matter how I felt when I went to Nat and Carol's house—good or bad—I always came away feeling better.

Mary and I would get together once in a while for a walk or for tea. It was wonderful to find someone willing to listen about TM, and I was so excited to tell her everything—how easy it was, how it had changed my life, and what a great vision Maharishi had for the world. She listened attentively, and would occasionally mention, "Oh, that sounds like something 'Abdu'l-Bahá would say." She gave me a few books, *The Hidden Words of Bahá'u'lláh* and *Paris Talks* by 'Abdu'l-Bahá, who was the son of Bahá'u'lláh, and whose name means the "Servant of the Glory." I glanced through them, and they all looked good. But I had TM after all, and was already a Christian. I didn't feel much need for a new religion. The next spring we said goodbye, as she was going back to Nicaragua to get married and run a banana plantation, and I was going to my icebreaker.

Whenever the ship returned home to Wilmington from our various deployments, I would occasionally travel up to Massachusetts to visit Bill. After a year or so he got serious with one of his roommates, Sandy, and they moved into a basement apartment in Sunderland, north of Amherst. Lucky for me, they had a spare bedroom, so I was able to intrude on them for a week or so, once or twice a year.

On one of these visits, walking through the center of Amherst, at the corner of Main and Pleasant streets, I looked up and there was Mary, hitchhiking. "Having any luck?" I asked. Her plans had fallen through, no marriage or banana plantation, and she was back at UMass to finish her studies. She re-introduced me to the Bahá'í community, and we had some more long talks.

That fall, after I got out of the Coast Guard and before going to MIU, I visited Bill and Sandy for a few weeks, and spent more time with Mary and the Bahá'ís. This Bahá'í Faith thing was getting interesting to me by now. At the end of a meeting at Nat and Carol's house, a question popped into my mind, and I asked them, "What is the relationship between Christ and Bahá'u'lláh, in Bahá'u'lláh's own words?"

"Oh," they replied. "You need to read *The Book of Certitude*. You can buy a copy at the bookstore in town."

I knew the bookstore, and went down the next day to buy *The Book of Certitude*. I took it back to Bill and Sandy's place and started reading. But I didn't understand a word. It was all English, and I always thought of myself as a pretty good reader, but the language was too lofty for me to comprehend. At the same time, I knew all of it was true. At one point it was talking about the Sun of Truth and I looked up, out the window, and saw the sun setting over the trees and houses across the field, a perfectly beautiful, crimson ball of fire, almost too brilliant to look upon. I took that as a sign.

MIU

Leaving my ship and arriving at MIU was like taking a rocket from Pluto and landing right in the sun. I was used to being the only one doing TM, and suddenly I was among the largest group of meditators in the world. My fellow students, the faculty, and the staff—from cooks to security guards—everyone did TM. My happiness knew no bounds.

The university was new, but the campus was not. Located in Fairfield, Iowa, on the north side of town, it was originally a Presbyterian institution, Parsons College. It had expanded rapidly during the Vietnam War, taking on hundreds of draft-dodging hopefuls, only to collapse into bankruptcy when the war ended. The international TM organization had picked it up at a bargain price when looking for a location in the mid-1970s. The old campus was located in a single block on the north side of town, with a few traditional-looking buildings, including a stone chapel, nestled among grassy lawns and large oak trees. The new campus comprised a large array of modern brick structures spreading north and west from there, many of which had been built rather hastily to house the large influx of students earlier in the decade.

Up on a hill, near the athletic field, sat the newly-finished Golden Dome. It was a beautiful structure. Its geodesic frame was constructed of laminated oak beams joined into interlocking triangles. These were covered by planks, except for six triangular skylights in the center of the dome. The planks were topped with foam for waterproofing and insulation, painted gold. All around the base of the dome were mirrored arched windows. Inside the dome was one huge space void of any walls or partitions except for a raised platform opposite the entry doors, that served as a stage. The vast concrete floor was completely covered with thick foam mats wrapped in white cloth. The foam was for flying.

Flying? Well, not exactly. Not when I was there, anyway. In the mid-70s, Maharishi had introduced the TM-Sidhi program. Based on the TM program, the TM-Sidhi program allows people to not only experience Transcendental Consciousness, but also to act within that state. The idea is that you put forth an intention to do or experience something while in the state of TC, and that intention gets realized, to whatever extent TC is stabilized in the nervous system. For those in whom the experience of TC is not so profound, doing the TM-Sidhi program helps to develop it more rapidly.

Among the various intentions and tasks included in the TM-Sidhi program, the most interesting and controversial is levitation. That is, during the state of TC, the mind has the intention of lifting off the ground, and the body lifts off the ground. Recently this has been called Yogic Flying® but when I was at MIU we called it the levitation or 'flying' part of the TM-Sidhi program. As the level of TC in most people was and is still developing, the experience has largely been that the body has the impulse to lift off the ground for a split second, and then drops back down. Hence the need for the foam mats in the dome. This was where the students, faculty, staff, and others in the TM community practiced the TM-Sidhi program.

I had first heard about the TM-Sidhi program back at the TM center in Cambridge. There I saw pictures of young people in loose-fitting clothes, with big smiles on their faces, sitting cross-legged about six to twelve inches in the air above foam pads covered with white cloth. A closer look suggested that these pictures may have been carefully chosen from a sequence of hopping, at the peak of each hop, to make it appear as if the person was hovering along towards the camera. I couldn't be sure, though. In any case, I told myself, if all of the other stuff is true, why not this?

So I was keen on learning the TM-Sidhi program, to become a Sidha. They had offered it to MIU students in the past, they told me, and might offer it in the summer. Meanwhile, all the Sidhas on campus meditated together for an hour or more, morning and evening. The men all went to the Men's Dome, and the ladies were in the fieldhouse until later that year when a second, Ladies' Dome was completed.

Being a Sidha brought you deeper into Maharishi's World Government of the Age of Enlightenment, in two ways. On an organizational level, everyone who did TM was considered a Citizen of the Age of Enlightenment, while meditators who did the TM-Sidhi program were known as Citizen-Sidhas.

TM teachers who were Sidhas and those involved in the TM organization were Governors of the Age of Enlightenment. Around the world in various countries there were Capitals of the Age of Enlightenment. One of those Capitals was on the MIU campus, and was responsible for administering TM courses like the TM and TM-Sidhi course instructions, residence courses, World Peace Assemblies, and others.

On another level, the World Government of the Age of Enlightenment was like no other government that I had ever heard of. It governed from the level of consciousness. In the 1970s, scientists working with Maharishi discovered that when a person does the TM technique, it affects the people around them. Like a pebble dropped in a pool, someone meditating enlivens the field of pure consciousness, and the effect radiates outwards. They conducted studies showing that if just 1% of a group of people meditated regularly, you would see measurable, positive changes in the surrounding environment, like a reduction in the crime rate or fewer hospitalizations. They called this the Maharishi Effect.

They also published numerous peer-reviewed articles in top scientific journals about the TM-Sidhi program, where the effect is much stronger. It only took the square root of 1% of the population to be doing the TM-Sidhi program together to get the same results. This was called the Super-Radiance Effect. One of the main goals of the World Government of the Age of Enlightenment was to establish world peace. The quickest way to achieve that was to establish a permanent group of Sidhas in one place in every country of the world, whose numbers equalled or exceeded the square root of 1% of the population of the country. For the USA, the number at that time was 1600. When I arrived at MIU, and the whole time I was there, that was the goal. And I wanted to be part of it.

Of course, I was there as a student as well. The curriculum was based on the Science of Creative Intelligence®, or SCI. The first course you took was simply SCI, consisting of 33 videotaped lessons of Maharishi explaining SCI, followed by discussion. For the rest of the first year, there were the Core Courses, each just a week or two long, covering every discipline—math, art, biology, physics, literature, chemistry, writing, business, music, religion, and more—all in the light of consciousness. Every discipline was shown to be an expression of the unified field of pure consciousness, which was later referred to as the Unified Field of Natural Law, or simply the Unified Field. That was the field that we experienced during the TM program, and the field that was enlivened during the TM-Sidhi program. All knowledge is connected to pure consciousness, and pure consciousness is connected to the Self. Hence, the university motto: Knowledge is structured in consciousness.

Following the first year, the second year had month-long, in-depth courses in the various major disciplines. The third and fourth years also had month-long courses, in traditional university majors like Physics, Business, Psychology, Education, and so on. A few days after I arrived they announced a new major, Natural Law, that would start that fall. There were not a lot of details available yet, but the idea was that the Natural Law degree would go deeply into Maharishi's teachings. That was just what I wanted. I immediately decided to major in Natural Law.

But first, the SCI course. Every day, morning and afternoon for four weeks, we listened as Maharishi talked on video tapes about creative intelligence—how it is the unchanging source of all change, the state of least excitation, the field of all possibilities, greater than the greatest and smaller than the smallest. We learned how TM allows us to experience that field, and live 200% of life, 100% of the relative, changing world, and 100% of the unbounded field of creative intelligence. We found out that in addition to the fourth and fifth states of consciousness, TC, and CC, there is a sixth state, God Consciousness or GC, where you gain celestial perception, and a seventh state, Unity Consciousness or UC, where you experience all of creation in terms of the unbounded Self.

I was ecstatic. I could barely contain myself. Every class was a mind-blowing experience. Walking out of the classroom after each lesson I would rave to my friends about what we had just learned, feeling like there could not possibly be anything more amazing. And yet the next class would take us even farther into this ever-expanding arena of knowledge. By the end of the month I felt like I had already learned several lifetimes of valuable knowledge, enough to satisfy me for all time. And yet things were just beginning.

A New Creation

During these explosive first few weeks at MIU, I noticed on the bulletin board in the dining room a poster advertising a Bahá'í fireside. "Why not?" I asked myself. "This is the place where all dreams come true, isn't it? Maybe I'll find some TM meditators who are Bahá'ís as well." I decided not to follow up until after completing the SCI course, since that was taking my full attention. There was a meeting announced for a Sunday in mid-February, which I decided to attend.

The meeting was in a home near the campus, but I got the address wrong, and spent almost an hour looking for the place. When I finally got there, they were just finishing up. The speaker, Roger, a TM teacher who was also a Bahá'í, was talking enthusiastically about prayer. He said that Bahá'ís have lots of prayers, and that some of them are obligatory, ones that Bahá'ís say every day. He showed us a prayer book and said they cost one dollar. That seemed like a reasonable price, so I bought one. He showed me a short obligatory prayer, and it didn't seem too difficult. I figured I could try saying that every day, to see what would happen. He was going to have another meeting the next Sunday, and invited me to come.

That meeting was in the girls dorm, in the room of a girl named Marie. In fact, the only people in the meeting were Marie, Roger, and myself. Roger was again speaking very enthusiastically, focusing all of his attention on Marie, reading different parts of the Bahá'í writings to illustrate and back up his thoughts. At one point he read this quote from Bahá'u'lláh:

> I testify that no sooner had the First Word proceeded, through the potency of Thy will and purpose, out of His mouth, and the First Call gone forth from His lips than the whole creation was revolutionized, and all that are in the heavens and all that are on earth were stirred to the depths. Through that Word the realities of all created things were shaken, were divided, separated, scattered, combined and reunited, disclosing, in both the contingent world and the heavenly kingdom, entities of a new creation, and revealing, in the unseen realms, the signs and tokens of Thy unity and oneness. Through that Call Thou didst announce unto all Thy servants the advent of Thy most great Revelation and the appearance of Thy most perfect Cause.[1]

As Roger read those words, my mind was flooded with images of everything coming apart and then being put back together, not in a physical sense, but in some kind of deeper, spiritual way. This was profound. It reminded me of Aslan in the Narnia books talking about the "Deeper Magic from Before the Dawn of Time."[2] It seemed eternal, and yet right now, pre-existing and yet ever-present. At that moment I realized that Bahá'u'lláh must be the Return of Christ!

The next day at lunch I saw Roger in the dining hall, and told him, "Bahá'u'lláh is the Man. I want to be a Bahá'í." He whisked me upstairs to a friend's dorm room and started telling me all about the Bahá'í Faith. He didn't know me, after all, and had no idea that I had any previous introduction or background knowledge. He wanted to tell me all about the Báb, 'Abdu'l-Bahá, the Covenant, the Guardian, the Universal House of Justice, Spiritual Assemblies, 19-Day Feasts, and all the rest. He warned me that the Fast would start in a few days. I kept saying, "Yes, yes, I know, I know, just sign me up." I was very conscious of the promise I had made to myself back in 5th grade—that if Christ ever returns, I wanted to be on his side. I didn't want any delays. Finally, Roger allowed me to sign a card that said that I believe in Bahá'u'lláh (the Glory of God) as the Manifestation of God for this age, and in His Forerunner, the Báb (the Gate), and in the Center of His Covenant, 'Abdu'l-Bahá (the Servant of the Glory); and also that Bahá'u'lláh has established institutions and laws which I must obey.

In the weeks and months that followed, Roger kept me well-informed about the Bahá'í Faith. He shared stories about working as a volunteer in the Bahá'í World Center in Haifa, Israel, for a year before he came to MIU. He told me that I had to pray every day, and read the Bahá'í writings morning and evening.

These writings are unique in the history of the world's religions because they were written by the Prophet Himself. The originals have been meticulously preserved at the Bahá'í

World Center. Comprising over 100 volumes' worth of books, tablets, letters, and prayers, they were revealed by the Báb and Bahá'u'lláh in Persian and Arabic. Many of them were first translated into English by Shoghi Effendi, the great-grandson of Bahá'u'lláh, and they are now available in hundreds of languages.

These writings are different from ordinary books. As they are the inspired Word of God, they are sometimes referred to as the Creative Word. Bahá'u'lláh wrote, "Every word that proceedeth out of the mouth of God is endowed with such potency as can instill new life into every human frame, if ye be of them that comprehend this truth."[3]

Like the Bahá'í Faith itself, the Bahá'í writings are both mystical and practical. Bahá'u'lláh instructed His followers to not just read them, but also to put them into action. He said, "It is incumbent upon every man of insight and understanding to strive to translate that which hath been written into reality and action."[4]

Now I had to read these writings every day. The easiest way possible, the most accessible book, was my copy of *The Hidden Words* that Mary had given me. Most passages were just a sentence or two. I started reading one passage in the morning and a second one in the evening. I also recited the shortest of the obligatory prayers every day. The verses of *The Hidden Words* were quite appealing; many of them pointing to a deeper reality that I was only dimly becoming aware of, through TM. For example, one of them says:

O Son of My Handmaid! Didst thou behold immortal sovereignty, thou wouldst strive to pass from this fleeting world. But to conceal the one from thee and to reveal the other is a mystery which none but the pure in heart can comprehend.[5]

That passage suggested to me the 200% of reality that Maharishi talked about in the SCI course. The "fleeting world" is the relative, changing world, and the "immortal sovereignty" corresponds to the realm of the Absolute, the unbounded field of creative intelligence. Why that was so well hidden, and why we are usually only aware of the relative world was indeed a mystery to me. Why not give everyone easy access to the Absolute? That's what Maharishi seemed to be doing.

Roger also encouraged me to learn more of the history of the Bahá'í Faith, to read in particular one book: *The Dawn Breakers*. This is an account of the life of the Báb and His early followers. Set in one of the darkest periods of the history of Iran, the Báb blazed out as bright as the morning sun, and set aflame the hearts of the pure souls that turned towards Him and followed Him. That same light of pure spirit frightened and repelled the corrupt government officials and religious leaders, who persecuted the Báb and His followers. Thousands were martyred, including the Báb Himself.

Reading their stories, the eye-witness accounts of the courage of these early "Bábis" (followers of the Báb), moved me deeply. Many of them had very little knowledge of the Báb's teachings, and because He was in prison most of the time, most of them had never even met Him. Yet they were willing to give their lives for His Cause. Their heads were cut off and put on spears, they were blown from the mouths of cannons, chained and branded, suffering every cruelty and indignity that their perverse tormentors could imagine. And yet, through it all, they remained calm and steadfast, never wavering in their faith.

This all seemed far removed from the ideal world that Maharishi was working to create. There was no systematic technique for the development of consciousness among the followers of the Báb. And yet somehow their faith was strong enough to bear witness to the reality of Divinity in Him, to the point where they willingly, in some cases eagerly, laid down their lives. Reading their stories, I deeply admired these early believers, and sometimes dared to hope that one day I too could have the chance to lay down my life in that way, to be a martyr, while also wondering whether I would have the courage and faith to do so, should that moment ever arrive.

That spring Roger was very active in teaching the Faith, and by May there were a total of nine of us, just enough to form a Local Spiritual Assembly. Roger arranged for a friend who lived in a nearby Bahá'í community to come and help us with the Assembly formation. With him came also Mrs. Khadem, the wife of the Hand of the Cause. At the time I had little understanding of the significance of what was happening, but

Roger was excited and pleased, and his spirit spread through all of us.

From these very humble beginnings, our little community had its ups and downs. Roger left MIU at the end of the semester, and for the summer we had nobody to really guide us. But in the fall, and every semester afterwards, we were blessed by one or more deepened Bahá'ís who could help us increase our knowledge and understanding of the Bahá'í Revelation, particularly in light of Maharishi's teachings.

In any event, that whole first summer my time was completely taken up with the TM-Sidhi course. It was a two-month rounding course in residence, with the instructions for the Sidhis included among all of the extra meditation sessions and Maharishi tapes. Like the TM program itself, the course content for the TM-Sidhi program is confidential. The reason for this is two-fold. First, the method of instruction is highly specialized, and they didn't want people thinking once they had learned the techniques, that they would be able to teach them. And second, every person's experience varies greatly, and you shouldn't talk about your experience because it might raise false expectations for others.

I can say that it was a very deep and profound course, and yet the practice of the Sidhis was as easy and effortless as TM. We learned the flying sutra near the end of the course, and for me it was amazing. It worked as described in the literature and promotional materials. Now I could join the other Sidhas in the dome for the daily Super-Radiance program. I felt connected. I felt like I was doing something uncommonly great for world peace, while experiencing growing inner peace and developing higher states of consciousness.

The core courses continued in the fall, and with the TM-Sidhi course complete, I had more time to devote to learning about the Bahá'í Faith, and even to spread the message, albeit in a hesitant sort of way. As a Christian, I had always resented the fundamentalists and Bible-thumpers who would challenge people with their sure knowledge that they were saved—and what about you? Plus, this was all new to me. So it took a little while before I could work up the courage to tell my friends that I had become a Bahá'í. The typical reply would be, in effect, "What? Bahá'í? What's that? Isn't Maharishi enough for you? Why do you need religion when you have the fullness of knowledge?" At first I didn't have answers for them. My friend Mark used to joke with me, greeting me by saying, "Bahá'í, B'hob, B'how you doin'?" ("Hi, Bob, how are you doing?") Oddly enough, being able to laugh at myself made things easier.

I put a poster on my door that said, "The source of all learning is the knowledge of God, exalted be His glory, and this cannot be attained save through the knowledge of His Divine Manifestation. - Bahá'u'lláh"[6] A few weeks later it had been removed. I figured it must have rubbed someone the wrong way. Then I put up one that said, "The potentialities inherent in the station of man, the full measure of his destiny on earth, the innate excellence of his reality, must all be manifested in this promised Day of God. - Bahá'u'lláh"[7] That must have struck a better chord, because it stayed up.

Although Roger was no longer around to shepherd us, some of us began to get together for 19-Day Feasts and Holy Days. Our conversations invariably turned towards comparisons between TM and the Bahá'í Faith, and then often on to all kinds of esoteric stuff. People at MIU were attracted to anything mystical. Typically the first book we would share with seekers would be *The Seven Valleys and The Four Valleys* by Bahá'u'lláh. People would flip through it and say, "OK, sure, that all makes sense. It sounds just like what Maharishi would say." Occasionally someone would want to know more, and once in a while an attracted soul would enroll as a Bahá'í.

Most people were not interested in religion, though. The prevailing attitude, particularly among TM teachers, Governors, and those who most deeply identified with the TM organization, was that TM was enough. In fact, for them TM was better than religion. After all, they would say, Jesus enlightened only 12 disciples, while Maharishi was going to enlighten the world. Despite this attitude, early on I discovered in Maharishi's teachings several important connections to religion.

For example, in the introduction to his commentary on the *Bhagavad-Gita*, he referred to it as the "Light of Life, lit by God at the altar of man, to save humanity from the darkness of ignorance and suffering."[8]

Also, the MIU catalog listed 16 versions of the Constitution of the World Government of the Age of Enlightenment, and the 15th was all of the sacred scriptures of all of the religions of the world.

Another example was in an audio tape that I heard, and often heard repeated, in which someone asked Maharishi, in effect, "OK, so I do my meditation and then plunge into daily activity. But what kind of activity is best for growing quickly towards enlightenment?"

"You should follow the teachings of your religion," Maharishi replied.

"But I don't have any religion," the questioner responded. "What should I do then?"

"Follow the guidance of your parents," was Maharishi's response.

"But I don't trust my parents. They set a very poor example," came the reply.

"Then do what you know to be right, and don't do what you know to be wrong," was Maharishi's final answer.

Unfortunately, too many meditators I knew jumped right to the third answer, modifying it slightly to simply "Do whatever you want." As a new Bahá'í, and as someone who wanted the quickest path to enlightenment, that seemed like a poor, and possibly dangerous approach. Why risk the chance of getting lost in the weeds when Bahá'u'lláh has spelled things out so clearly, I reasoned.

The thing is, MIU students came from all backgrounds and all walks of life. At times it felt like the only thing we had in common was the TM technique. For most of us, TM was by far the most positive thing that had happened in our lives. And yet, that meant different things to different people. Some just did TM because it made them feel good, and had come to MIU for a good education. Others looked to Maharishi as their guru, and devoted themselves to him and the TM organization. Many of the teachers and Governors were in that category. Still others saw TM as a jumping-off point for all kinds of new-age and esoteric pursuits, from reflexology, iridology, strange diets, and kundalini yoga to astrology, crystal therapy, and even sharpening razor blades by putting them under a pyramid. Nothing was off the table for them.

In fact, for better or for worse, many people categorized the Bahá'í Faith as one of these additional "techniques" that got added to the TM program. This caused significant misunderstandings. We Bahá'ís often found ourselves challenged to present the Faith and its teachings in a way that addressed the fears on one hand, and the expectations on the other. We had to make clear that this was not some kind of contrived addition to the TM program—it was a legitimate, full-fledged religion. To their credit, the MIU faculty and administration showed little if any prejudice on this matter. They treated the Bahá'í Faith as simply a religion, always with respect, in my experience. We had a university-approved Bahá'í Club with a faculty advisor that maintained a bulletin board of activities for all religions, and we hosted weekly devotional meetings in the on-campus chapel.

For me, the Bahá'í Faith was a protection from all sorts of strange ideas and claims that circulated unofficially at MIU. Once I obtained a copy of the Urantia book, a description of the heavenly realms and inhabitants, purportedly channelled to a person by angels. It seemed pretty amazing at first. But I couldn't find any reference to Bahá'u'lláh in it. Since it was written in the 1950s, and whoever wrote it claimed all of this divine knowledge, it should have mentioned Bahá'u'lláh somewhere, I thought. But it didn't. It began to dawn on me that perhaps this Bahá'í thing was different, and deeper, than any of these kinds of supposedly esoteric knowledge.

That feeling became stronger the more I associated with people who had various "spiritual" interests and abilities. For example, my friend Dave often had a far-away look in his eye. He was able to read auras and see celestial beings, like angels and so on. He would occasionally describe them for me. I couldn't be completely sure if he was telling the truth, or just making it all up, but it didn't really matter. When it came to me telling him about Bahá'u'lláh, he wasn't interested. Then I realized how lucky I was to be able to recognize the truth of this Cause. My friend, with all of his ability to see angels, had somehow missed it completely. This kind of thing started me questioning the relationship between faith on the one hand, and the experience of higher states of consciousness, which the TM program develops, on the other.

Notes

1. Bahá'u'lláh, *Prayers and Meditations*, CLXXVIII

2. C.S. Lewis, *The Lion, the Witch, and the Wardrobe*, p 142

3. Bahá'u'lláh, *Gleanings from the Writings of Bahá'u'lláh*, LXXIV

4. Ibid, CXVII

5. Bahá'u'lláh, *The Hidden Words*, Persian #41

6. Bahá'u'lláh, *Tablets of Bahá'u'lláh*, p 156

7. Bahá'u'lláh, *Gleanings from the Writings of Bahá'u'lláh*, CLXII

8. Maharishi Mahesh Yogi, *Bhagavad-Gita - A New Translation and Commentary*, p 13

Natural Law and the Vedas

By the fall of 1982, I had completed the first and second year core course requirements and was ready to begin my major: Natural Law. For the next two years I dove deeply into Western science and Vedic Science^{SM}, or Maharishi's knowledge. This was as close as you could get to the TM teacher training course without actually being on that course. I felt privileged. Now I was going to find out: Where does TM come from, really? And how does it work, really?

The whole course, in fact the whole MIU education, was structured like a giant rounding course. There was a daily program, and we were encouraged to follow it. This meant doing asanas and pranayam in our dorm rooms, going to the domes for the TM-Sidhi program, then breakfast, followed by class. After a break for lunch, more classes. Then back to the domes for afternoon meditation, followed by dinner. There was an hour or two for homework, and then in bed, lights out, by 10 p.m.

Following the program closely and comfortably was the best, the quickest way to get to enlightenment. That was my goal, and I stuck to it firmly. There was time on Saturday afternoons for doing laundry and running errands, and on

Sundays for Bahá'í activities. But for the most part it was meditate, study, eat and sleep.

The Natural Law courses were in one-month blocks, with the added feature of daily classes in Sanskrit, the language of the Vedas. The blocks alternated between science subjects like physics, chemistry, and psychology with lectures given by top scientists in the field, or month-long videotape courses given by Maharishi. The intellectual knowledge was balanced by experiential knowledge in the dome. Our meditation was part of the curriculum. They took attendance in the dome and we earned course credit in Research into Consciousness. All of this reflected Maharishi's approach to the study of Natural Law, which was based on his understanding and experience of the Vedas.

The Vedas are as old as time. They are the song of creation. It is the song of the Self, singing to the Self, by its Self, through the Self. Because this song flows through everything, it flows through us. If someone's nervous system is refined enough, they can perceive the Vedas, because they are structured in pure consciousness. People who are able to perceive the Vedas are called "seers" or "rishis". The perception of the Vedas is often called "Vedic cognition." The Vedic rishis would go deeply into their own consciousness, and hear the song, and cognize the verses of the Vedas. This is the true origin of Vedic literature, according to Maharishi.

One spring the whole student body was invited to the Golden Dome, where we spent hours over a period of several days listening to special lectures that Maharishi had taped, regarding these verses of the Rig Veda:

Richo ak-share parame vyoman
Yasmin devâ adhi vishve nishedu,
Yastanna veda kim richâ karishyati
Ya it tad vidu sta ime samasate.[1]

Maharishi translated these verses as follows:

Richo ak-share parame vyoman
The verses of the Veda exist in the collapse of fullness
(the kshara of 'A') in the transcendental field,

Yasmin devâ adhi vishve nishedu,
In which reside all the Devas, the impulses of
creative intelligence, the laws of nature
responsible for the whole manifest universe.

Yastanna veda kim richâ karishyati
He whose awareness is not open to this field,
what can the verses accomplish for him?

Ya it tad vidu sta ime samasate.
Those who know this level of reality
are established in evenness, wholeness of life.

We repeated those verses over and over again, in Sanskrit and in English until we knew them by heart. To this day I can recite them word for word.

The first verse describes the mechanics of creation within the realm of pure consciousness, when fullness collapses to the value of a point, much as a quantum wave function collapses at the moment that a measurement is taken.

The second verse says that within this abstract realm are all of the lively impulses of consciousness, the laws of nature, that are responsible for the whole manifest universe.

The third verse talks about the need to refine our consciousness to truly understand the Vedas. Our awareness needs to be open to the pure field of creative intelligence, the source of Natural Law, the source of the Vedas. If we do not have the experience of pure consciousness, the Vedas have no meaning.

And the fourth verse affirms that if we are established at that level of reality, then the Vedas do have meaning, profound meaning, and we live that reality in evenness, wholeness, a state of enlightenment.

This understanding of the Vedas was revolutionary, and still is today. Virtually no Western scholar sees it this way, and probably few in India as well, except for those influenced by Maharishi. Equally revolutionary was Maharishi's approach to share this knowledge with the world through the TM program, and later the TM-Sidhi program. His mission was to bring about a revival of Vedic knowledge in its pure form. He called it Maharishi Vedic Science^{SM}.

Part of Maharishi's genius was to couch the study of the Vedas in the language of science, and to use the tools of science to study it. This brought it out of the realm of hand-waving and debate and into the laboratory. Scientific studies of all kinds were done on meditators, and virtually all of them produced significant results. Many were published in leading scientific journals, and have been collected and published in a number of volumes.

In the Natural Law program, we studied the deepest principles of physics and other disciplines, and saw that they were the same as the principles that govern our own consciousness, that we experienced during our meditation in the dome. That's why it was called "Research into Consciousness." While some of the students at MIU were more interested in pursuing career options, we in our major were caught up in the awe and wonder of natural law.

In chemistry we learned how a supersaturated solution can quickly change from a liquid to a crystal when a seed crystal is introduced. The molecules in a highly agitated, disorganized state suddenly take on the smooth organization of the crystal, and align themselves in perfect orderly patterns. We saw how this is similar to how our mind goes from disorderly thoughts to pure consciousness through the introduction of the mantra during meditation, as well as how a relatively small but coherent group of meditators or Sidhas can have a profound, phase-transition effect on the collective consciousness of an entire city or nation.

In physics we studied the cutting-edge super-symmetry and unified field theories being developed at CERN in Switzerland at the time. These were closely related to Maharishi's discussions of the pure field of creative intelligence, or what came to be referred to as the "Unified Field of Natural Law" that we experienced and enlivened during the TM-Sidhi program.

In mathematics, one casual remark from the professor cleared up a frustrating mental block about approaching a limit I had felt in calculus class back at Penn State. I couldn't get an intuitive grasp of the concept. How can you get continually closer and closer to something and never reach it? I wondered back then...could I ever get there?

"Of course," our Natural Law professor said, "the intuitive notion of approaching a limit is like transcending. The mind experiences finer and finer levels of a thought, until you transcend that thought and experience pure, unbounded consciousness." Wow. There it was. As simple as that. We can reach it. We actually can cross those limits, step over the boundary, and have the direct experience of infinity within our seemingly limited minds.

Notes

1. *Rig Veda* 1.164.39

Fully Engaged

I don't know exactly when it started, perhaps back in high school, or even earlier. I came to crave full engagement—the total experience. When reading a book, I would become the main character. Watching a movie, I was all in. Listening to music meant turning up the volume, closing my eyes, and being swept away. In the physical world the closest I came to full engagement was sailing, and especially racing. It was beauty in motion, communing with nature, a live, interacting chessboard of strategy, physical exertion, mental calculations, instinctive decisions—a ride on the wind and waves, and an occasional whack of water in the face. Thoughts and intentions translated swiftly into actions, and the results were immediate and obvious. There were no yardsticks. You needed to feel the pull on the tiller, the shifting gusts of wind, the subtle curves of the sails, and the slap of the hull against the waves to know if you were really getting every possible ounce of speed.

I wanted full engagement in the Coast Guard. I wanted the whole thing, every experience. I wanted to be on the water, handling towlines, taking the helm, checking the charts, scanning the horizon. I wanted to be manning lighthouses, hauling buoys, patrolling for smugglers, exploring the Arctic, and saving lives.

When I found TM, my drive for full engagement led me to MIU, and when I got there, I wanted the full experience. That, to me, was natural law. And in the Natural Law major, I found out what the truly full experience can be: Brahman Consciousness.

Hour upon hour, day after day, we would listen to Maharishi describe the experience of Brahman Conscious-ness. It was the fullness of life, the breath of creation flowing through you and the universe in an unbounded eternal state of ecstasy. It was more than you could possibly imagine, greater than any dream or fantasy, more real than the table in front of you, and yet hidden somewhere deep within. You touched upon it every time you meditated, and would occasionally experience a fleeting glimpse out of the corner of your eye, or even feel a wave of perfection wash over you when drifting into or out of sleep. For me, Brahman Consciousness was the goal. We talked about it, longed for it, even joked about it, until it became something so familiar, so pleasant to look forward to, although always remaining somehow far beyond our grasp.

I even found what I believed to be references to Brahman Consciousness in the writings of Bahá'u'lláh. He said: "Turn thy sight unto thyself, that thou mayest find Me standing within thee, mighty, powerful and self-subsisting."[1] He also said:

Whensoever the light of the revelation of the King of Oneness settleth upon the throne of the heart and soul, His radiance becometh visible in every limb and member. At that time, the mystery of the famed tradition gleameth out of the darkness: "A servant is drawn unto Me in prayer until I answer him, and when I have answered him, I become the ear wherewith he heareth ..." For thus the Master of the house hath appeared within His home, and all the pillars of the dwelling are ashine with His light. And as the action and effect of the light are from the Light-Giver, so it is that all move through Him and arise by His will.[2]

And then one day it happened. Totally unprepared, following the instructions of the TM-Sidhi program, it was as if I had stepped through a door into my heart, which suddenly turned inside out and my whole being became one with the universe and the heavens. It was as if on every side was a door which held the knowledge of all things. Looking back, perhaps the best way to describe it would be like the time I smuggled a glass jar into the local swimming pool. When I pushed it under water, it immediately disappeared. I could no longer see it. It became the whole swimming pool. And that was me, for maybe five minutes.

During that time I knew that this experience could not last. My nervous system was not strong enough, not pure enough, not developed enough to sustain such an experience for long.

I knew that this was just a glimpse, nowhere near the full integration of Brahman Consciousness that Maharishi talked about. But the time I was given was more than enough. I now knew, without a shadow of doubt, that in words sometimes attributed to Maharishi's teacher, Guru Dev, this was "the whole thing, the real thing."

Walking out of the dome, greeting my friends and other Sidhas and Governors, everything seemed "normal" again. But I was bursting with this knowledge of what is possible, what is real, what is so beyond anything that this mundane physical world has to offer. How many of these people know this, I wondered. How can we just be standing around or doing our daily tasks, knowing that this reality underlies everything? How can we possibly not give up everything to attain it?

Notes

1. Bahá'u'lláh, *The Hidden Words*, Arabic #13
2. Bahá'u'lláh, *The Call of the Divine Beloved*, pp 31-32

Communicating

As my time in the Natural Law major came to an end, and graduation drew near, I began thinking about what to do next. More than anything else, I wanted to share with the world what I had discovered, particularly with children and young people. If, as a child, I had known what I knew now, I would not have spent ten years of my life in confusion, questioning and searching. What was needed now was the ability to convey these precious answers to others.

One day, Dr. Pearson, head of the first-year writing workshop that changed my attitude towards writing, came up to me and told me about a new program to be introduced at MIU, Master in Professional Writing. The idea was to gain the skills needed for writing books, magazine articles, film scripts, technical documentation and more. It would start in one year. Would I be interested?

Would I? Absolutely! I took a year break from my studies and worked as a volunteer on MIU staff. Then in 1985 I enrolled with about a dozen other aspiring writers as the first students in the Professional Writing program.

Computers were rare in classrooms in those days, but we were each required to buy an Apple Macintosh, a revolutionary, new, easy-to-use computer. We were state of the art, on the cutting edge, and soon began desktop publishing a newspaper for the university, the MIU Review. Our professor, Dr. Karpen, had earned his PhD. in English doing basic research on "hypertext," a way to link writing electronically, which in a few short years would be known as the "HT" in HTML documents so commonly used on the World Wide Web. But the Internet was still off in the future. Our courses were focused on getting published in print media.

My area of interest was in sharing all the things I had learned at MIU, particularly in the sciences and natural law. I thought I could write science textbooks that introduced quantum theory and other advanced topics to young people, to show them what an amazing world we live in. I also wanted to introduce them, in a simple way, to the possibilities of higher states of consciousness, and that they had huge potential. We were all sending out query letters and magazine article proposals. I submitted a story to Highlights for Children called "Think Like a Scientist," and wrote a book proposal titled "You Make Math." As with the rest of my colleagues, few of these were accepted, but we were learning the ropes.

In addition to the sciences and natural law, I became interested in writing on Bahá'í themes. In scriptwriting class I submitted a video script about pilgrimage to the Bahá'í World Center. For our Vedic Literature class, I created and documented a Unified Field Chart for the Bahá'í Faith titled "A Glimpse of the Bahá'í Revelation through the window of

Vedic Science," which was well received. But the idea that most captured my heart and mind was to write a book about the Bahá'í Faith and TM.

By this time the Bahá'í community at MIU had grown a bit, and several well-deepened Bahá'ís who were also Sidhas or Governors were now at MIU or living nearby in the Fairfield community. Our conversations about TM and the Bahá'í Faith continued apace. We often compared the Bahá'í writings to Maharishi's teachings. Usually we found them to be compatible, but we could also see how misunderstandings might easily arise. I thought it would be good to write all of this down in a book. The book would explain the Bahá'í Faith to meditators, as well as explain TM to Bahá'ís.

Often at MIU, from the time I became a Bahá'í, I felt as if I was living between two vast systems of knowledge. Each had a profound vision of the world, of spirituality, and of the high station of humanity. Each had a bold plan for bringing into being a bright future for all of us. Each could point to amazing successes. Sometimes at the beach you might see, after a wave breaks, two parts of it rushing towards the shore, fanning out to intersect. At the point where they join, the speed is doubled. That's how I felt much of the time. And I thought maybe others would like to know about this, to share the joy.

So I sent a book proposal to the Bahá'í Publishing Trust in India, and got a positive response. Send it in, they said. I started writing an outline, and several chapters. But something wasn't quite right. Was I in over my head? How could I possibly explain all of this? In a long conversation with one of my Bahá'í friends, he said, "You think the Bahá'í Faith and TM are compatible, but that's just your opinion. You can't prove it. A lot of people think otherwise." And in a way, he was right. I believed in my heart they were compatible. I looked for the points of agreement, and found them. Yet many people looked for points of conflict, and found them as well.

Moreover, there was probably not a big audience for such a book. In fact, many times during those years, I felt that if I told the Bahá'ís everything I knew and believed about TM, some would get pretty upset. On the other hand, if I proclaimed all the things that I understood to be true about the Bahá'í Faith at MIU, many would not be pleased to hear it. To stay on the safe side, I decided to hold off on writing that book.

While pondering the question of how all the pieces might fit together, I began to see that there were indeed things people could object to. Taking Maharishi's teachings at face value, you could perceive conflicts on at least three important topics: union with God, fear of God, and the presence of God in His creation. Whether or not I wrote my book, I hoped for some clarity on these. And I had a deeper question as well.

So I wrote a letter to Maharishi. I briefly explained the three questions, with quotes from his commentary on the *Bhagavad-Gita*, and his book *The Science of Being and Art of Living*, comparing them to quotes from the Bahá'í writings that appeared to be saying the opposite. This was a prelude to the question that I had pondered for several years there at MIU. At the end of the letter I asked Maharishi: "Do you recognize Bahá'u'lláh as God's Messenger for this age?"

Then I explained why I asked such a personal question. I was facing a dilemma. If he recognized Bahá'u'lláh, why did he not say so? And if he did *not* recognize Him, then what is the use of being enlightened? Because Bahá'u'lláh has written:

> The first duty prescribed by God for His servants is the recognition of Him Who is the Dayspring of His Revelation and the Fountain of His laws, Who represen-teth the Godhead in both the Kingdom of His Cause and the world of creation. Whoso achieveth this duty hath attained unto all good; and whoso is deprived thereof hath gone astray, though he be the author of every righteous deed.[1]

Thus, is it possible to experience higher states of consciousness and not recognize the Manifestation of God? How could someone in that purified state not instantly acknowledge and accept, as soon as they found out about Him?

I did not receive a written answer. But a reply did come to me—two replies in fact, as I understand it. A few weeks after sending the letter, the head of the philosophy department joined me as I was walking to class. He asked a few questions, and then shared a few thoughts and insights on philosophy, meditation, and religion. He didn't mention the letter, but I felt that was the reason he approached me, most likely at the behest of someone who must have read it. He offered little more than what I would expect from someone representing the TM organization, but he was cordial and kind, and I appreciated him reaching out.

Around that same time, Maharishi appeared to me in a dream, one of only two times that I can remember such an occurrence. In the dream I was sitting with everyone in the dome, meditating. Maharishi came up to me. He didn't say anything, just handed me a bag of Amrit Kalash™. This was an Ayurvedic substance that was being recommended in those days for enhancing experiences of higher states of consciousness. The message I got was this: Maharishi provides the experience.

That message brought to mind this passage from *The Book of Certitude*:

> A Revelation, of which the Prophets of God, His saints and chosen ones, have either not been informed, or which, in pursuance of God's inscrutable Decree, they have not disclosed...[2]

Certain reliable friends had informed me that Maharishi was aware of the Bahá'í Revelation. His role, as I saw it, was to bring TM to the world, to revive the Vedas. It occurred to me that he could not have been so effective at that, and people would not have understood it as well, had he also been actively proclaiming the Bahá'í Faith. In fact, many listeners may well have rejected him and his message altogether. And so I chose and still choose to believe that he is one of those who, in keeping with God's decree, has not disclosed this Revelation.

Notes

1. Bahá'u'lláh, *Kitáb-i-Aqdas (Most Holy Book)*, p 19
2. Bahá'u'lláh, *Kitáb-i-Íqán (The Book of Certitude)*, p 244

Moving On

Whether by coincidence or as a result of the Super-Radiance Effect, by the middle of the 1980s we started to witness a growing awareness of the need and possibility of world peace. The Universal House of Justice of the Bahá'í Faith released a statement in 1985 titled, *The Promise of Word Peace*, saying that peace among nations is not only possible, but inevitable. The United Nations declared 1986 as the Year of World Peace.

Maharishi himself declared 1987 to be The Year of World Peace. For several decades, he had been giving a name to each year, such as 1959 - The Year of Global Awakening, or 1969 - The Year of Supreme Knowledge, or 1977 - The Year of Ideal Society. Now this was The Year of World Peace. He had previously laid out the various criteria for world peace, and that year he proclaimed them as having been fulfilled.

I was elated! World peace was finally here—at least from Maharishi's perspective. One of my motives in coming to MIU was to become a Sidha, to join the Super-Radiance program in the dome, and to help bring about world peace. We were constantly encouraged to do our TM-Sidhi program in the dome, and were often reminded that this was the key to world peace. Now it seemed that world peace was finally here. Maybe now we could relax a little bit.

Near the end of the Professional Writing program I was offered a full-time writing job, editing and publishing a technical newsletter and marketing materials for Unifield Natural Gas Group. I moved to an apartment in town and joined the Town Super-Radiance program. We sometimes meditated in the dome, but usually in a new fieldhouse built to handle the overflow, because our numbers were increasing.

Fairfield was a great place to live. I had always felt very much at home at MIU and with the meditating community. Now on my new job, living off-campus, no longer attending classes, life settled into a different kind of routine. The work was interesting and challenging enough, although I was no longer right on the cutting edge of Maharishi's knowledge.

That knowledge had certainly changed my life. When I first applied to MIU, my goal had been to become a TM teacher, to share this wonderful meditation technique and knowledge with everyone. After accepting Bahá'u'lláh, during the subsequent years at MIU, although I still treasured the TM program, I began feeling my identity shifting away from the TM organization and more towards the Bahá'í Faith. Our Bahá'í community was growing deeper in our faith and understanding, and my world paradigm was taking on a more Bahá'í perspective. I had been regularly attending Iowa summer schools and unit conventions, and started travelling now to national events as well. In the summer of 1988, I drove with some friends to the National Bahá'í Youth Conference in Indiana, and attended a workshop on pioneering.

Pioneering! It meant moving to a new place, often a new country, to teach the Faith and support growing communities of Bahá'ís. It was a little like being a missionary, except that you didn't get a salary—you had to find your own work. Since being a martyr was not a realistic option for me, this was the closest to the full Bahá'í experience I could hope to get. At the conference I made a pledge to be out of the USA, at a pioneering post, before the end of 1989.

A new mission, a broader purpose, wider horizons. The experiences, the support of nature, the confirmations received, the opportunities for service and growth that came through this new pioneering adventure and those to follow could fill another book. Throughout it all, I continued meditating regularly, and kept stored away in the back of my mind an unfinished task.

That task was to put down in writing my understanding of the relationship between the TM program and the Bahá'í Faith. I needed to clarify in my own mind what seemed to be two independent spiritual paths. Are these somehow related to each other? The decades away from MIU have given me a deeper understanding of what it means to be a Bahá'í, and what guidance may be derived from the Bahá'í writings on this subject. After so much time, it seems that the opportunity has finally come to put down some thoughts in writing. These I share with you in the second part of this book, Reflections.

Part 2. Reflections

Evaluation

TM for me has always been something of a miracle—a daily miracle. From the time I first learned TM, the thought was in the back of my mind: This is so good, somehow it must be from God. But how? Part of my deepening in experience and understanding of TM at MIU, as well as before and since, was a quest to investigate this feeling, and to find out more. Now it seems the time has come to share some of what I've discovered. My approach is to consider my own experience and what I have learned about the TM program and Maharishi's revival of Vedic knowledge, and to show how it might come from God, as well as bring us closer to God, based on guidance from the Bahá'í writings.

First off, to the best of my knowledge, we can take Maharishi and the TM organization at their word that TM is not a religion. You don't have to believe in anything for it to work. The TM and TM-Sidhi programs are as advertised —simple, natural, effortless techniques for developing and stabilizing the experience of higher states of consciousness. They are based in Maharishi's deep understanding and systematic revival of Vedic Science. Maharishi viewed the Vedic literature not as something merely to be believed, but rather a truth that can be lived. For him, the Vedas are to be investigated through the experience of pure consciousness, and can in turn be applied to cultivate that experience.

Justice, according to Bahá'u'lláh, will allow us to see with our own eyes, to seek out the truth, to come to our own understanding. He asks: "How can ye judge a matter whereof ye have no knowledge?"[1] Maharishi points out that you cannot imagine the taste of a strawberry until you taste it. Thus, until we understand TM and Vedic Science through the experience of pure consciousness, the pure field of creative intelligence, we are in no position to judge. You must at least learn TM to properly evaluate it. Nevertheless, before taking such a step, we can use the guidance of the Bahá'í writings to get some idea of whether such investigation may be worthwhile. And for those who have learned TM, this guidance may be helpful to address any questions that might arise, and to deepen understanding.

Bahá'u'lláh has established standards for discerning truth from error. He said, "Verily this is that Most Great Beauty, foretold in the Books of the Messengers, through Whom truth shall be distinguished from error and the wisdom of every command shall be tested."[2] These standards are found in the writings of the Báb and Bahá'u'lláh, as well as their authorized interpreters, 'Abdu'l-Bahá and Shoghi Effendi. We can apply the standards given in these writings to questions regarding the source, validity, and value of the TM program, and whether it might ultimately come from God.

Some common claims often made of Transcendental Meditation are that it is natural, practical, beneficial, verifiable, and universal. Let's take a look at each one of these.

Natural

The TM technique is a simple, natural, effortless process that allows the mind to settle down, providing deep rest to the body. It is so easy that anyone can do it, and you begin to experience the benefits from the very first day. In fact, TM is so easy that if you try, you are doing it wrong. It follows the natural tendency of the mind to always seek more. For me, and for any TM meditator that I've ever talked to, TM has always been easy and natural.

Some may ask, "If TM is natural, why does it need to be learned?" Well, there are many things in life that need to be learned, even though they are natural. Language is one of them. Social behavior is another—learning how to give and receive love. This need for an educator is natural, according to 'Abdu'l-Bahá. He said, "When we consider existence, we observe that the mineral, the vegetable, the animal, and the human realms, each and all, are in need of an educator. ... If a man is left alone in a wilderness where he sees none of his own kind, he will undoubtedly become a mere animal. It is therefore clear that an educator is needed."[3]

The laws of nature are very deep, very profound. We are only beginning to understand them. Albert Einstein saw nature as an elegant structure, one that is revealed by science. Bahá'u'lláh has written, "Nature is God's Will and is its expression in and through the contingent world."[4] To me this suggests that if TM is natural, it somehow conforms to God's Will. If we are living more and more in accord with natural law, somehow we must be living more and more in accord with God's Will.

Practical

There are two aspects of the TM program: meditation and action. Maharishi uses an analogy of dying cloth. Back in the old days, in India, they would dye cloth by first putting it into a vat of dye, where it would gain a deep, rich color. Then they would spread it out in the sun, causing the color to almost completely fade away. They would put it back in the dye, and back into the sun many times. Eventually the color would stabilize, and never fade again.

This is how the TM program works. During meditation the mind gains the experience of pure consciousness, and during activity that experience mostly fades away. But through repeated cycles of deep rest and dynamic activity the mind becomes more and more capable of maintaining a deep sense of calm even during the most dynamic activity. Thus there are two interdependent aspects of growth towards enlightenment: deep rest and dynamic activity.

This kind of balance between meditation and action was expressed in a letter written on behalf of Shoghi Effendi, which states, "Prayer and meditation are very important factors in deepening the spiritual life of the individual, but with them must go also action and example, as these are the tangible results of the former. Both are essential."[5]

Beneficial

The TM program offers many benefits. Some of these include deep relief from stress, clarity of mind, and improved health. Negative tendencies like anxiety, depression, insomnia, drug and alcohol abuse decrease over time, while intelligence, creativity, learning ability, perception, and memory blossom and flourish. Studies show changes in personality as well, including increased spontaneity, inner control, tolerance and sociability, along with greater emotional stability and job satisfaction. In short, almost any positive trait or characteristic that people have been able to identify has been shown to improve in people practicing TM.

Although it might seem obvious that good things come from God, the Bahá'í writings affirm this. Bahá'u'lláh wrote, "Every good thing is of God..."[6] He also wrote, "In this glorious Day whatever will purge you from corruption and will lead you towards peace and composure, is indeed the Straight Path."[7] Given all of the benefits of the TM program, including the way that it releases stress, cleanses the nervous system, and provides peace of mind, these quotes reassure me that it is indeed of God, a good path.

In fact, Bahá'u'lláh enjoins us to hold to the good: "O peoples of the world! Forsake all evil, hold fast that which is good."[8] If something is beneficial, if it is good, it is clearly acceptable to God. We should hold on to it.

Verifiable

Maharishi says that there are three ways that we can verify the TM and TM-Sidhi programs—through personal experience, science, and tradition.

Verified through Personal Experience

The first validation of TM that Maharishi offers is our own experience. The proof of the pudding is in the eating. I know from my experience that TM works. I have experienced the benefits in my own life. All the people I know who have learned TM—even those who for some reason have stopped meditating—have said that they experienced benefits, to a greater or lesser degree. Not surprisingly, few if any clearly experienced higher states of consciousness right away. Maharishi doesn't promise that. What he does say is that you will gain the benefits, and over time you will grow in your experience of pure consciousness.

Bahá'u'lláh teaches that we must independently investigate the truth. He counsels us to "look into all things with a searching eye."[9] He also wrote, "One must, then, read the book of one's own self."[10] Each one of us needs to find truth for ourselves, not through imitation or knowledge that we blindly accept from others. 'Abdu'l-Bahá said:

> God has not intended man to imitate blindly his fathers and ancestors. He has endowed him with mind, or the faculty of reasoning, by the exercise of which he is to investigate and discover the truth, and that which he finds real and true he must accept. He must not be an imitator or blind follower of any soul. He must not rely implicitly upon the opinion of any man without investigation; nay, each soul must seek intelligently and independently, arriving at a real conclusion and bound only by that reality.[11]

Thus, the ultimate validation is through our own experience. Before we reach that point, we may need some indication that such a thing is worth investigating at all. That's where the testimony of others may play a role, as well as scientific validation and a long tradition of masters.

Verified through Science

Scientific inquiry on the beneficial effects of the TM program is exhaustive. It is probably the most studied meditation technique in the world. Research has been conducted in leading academic and research facilities such as Harvard Medical School, Yale Medical School, Stanford Medical School, and the Medical College of Georgia. Hundreds of articles have been published in more than 150 scientific journals detailing peer-reviewed research on TM. Many of these papers have been collected and published in eight volumes titled: *Scientific Research on Transcendental Meditation and TM-Sidhi Program.*

A fundamental principle of the Bahá'í Faith is that truth must conform with science and reason. 'Abdu'l-Bahá said "Put all your beliefs into harmony with science; there can be no opposition, for truth is one."[12]

For Bahá'ís, science is acknowledged as a valid means for discovering truth. 'Abdu'l-Bahá said, "Science must be accepted. No one truth can contradict another truth. Light is good in whatsoever lamp it is burning!"[13]

We should thus apply this criteria when deciding whether a meditation technique is valid, thereby avoiding superstition and human error. Shoghi Effendi, also known as the Guardian of the Bahá'í Faith, affirms this approach. "Meditation is very important, and the Guardian sees no reason why the friends should not be taught to meditate, but they should guard against superstitious or foolish ideas creeping into it."[14]

So, to whatever degree the TM program offers scientific evidence for its validity, to that degree we can be assured that it is true, and thus acceptable in the sight of God.

Verified through Vedic Tradition

The third means of verification is through the Vedic Tradition, which Maharishi explains:

> The Vedic Tradition, upheld in its purity by a long history of custodians, enshrines the supreme knowledge of the integration of life. From time to time a revival of man's understanding of the eternal wisdom of this Holy Tradition arises to rescue him from suffering, restoring him to the speedy path of evolution, and awakening him to a meaningful life in fulfilment. The Masters of this Tradition have been exponents of reality from earliest ages. In each new epoch, they have propounded the enduring truths of practical living and have set out those standards by which men's lives may attain the highest achievements and fulfillment, generation after generation.[15]

This revival of the Vedic Tradition has cleared up many superstitions and superficial interpretations of the Vedas which are commonly assumed to be true. Erroneous ideas were handed down from one generation to the next with little understanding of the source or meaning of the Vedas. People came to view Vedic literature as imaginative stories, and many superstitions arose. In contrast, Maharishi's teacher, Guru Dev, began a revival of the profound knowledge of the Vedas, and how it is based in pure consciousness. Maharishi developed this approach, and shared it with the world. The

Vedic Tradition, from this perspective, is as old as the Vedas themselves, brought to light through Maharishi's revival.

Bahá'u'lláh affirms that our current knowledge can be based on more profound knowledge from an earlier time. He says:

> Although it is recognized that the contemporary men of learning are highly qualified in philosophy, arts and crafts, yet were anyone to observe with a discriminating eye he would readily comprehend that most of this knowledge hath been acquired from the sages of the past, for it is they who have laid the foundation of philosophy, reared its structure and reinforced its pillars.[16]

There is more to this that we will discuss later, in the Origins chapter. For now, suffice it to say that Maharishi did not invent the TM program from himself. Rather, he brought to light the deep truths of the Vedic Tradition that were entrusted to him by his teacher, Guru Dev.

Universal

The TM program is for everyone—rich, poor, young, old, students, professionals, soldiers, housewives, even convicts. The age of instruction is ten years old or older, with a special program for children ages five through nine.

Bahá'u'lláh said, "Let your vision be world-embracing, rather than confined to your own self."[17] In the prime of his life, Maharishi left his reclusive abode in northern India, travelled to the south, and began teaching Transcendental Meditation. Seeing the interest and demand, he then began travelling around the world, teaching TM and organizing a movement. He developed a system for training teachers, creating the means to teach thousands and eventually hundreds of thousands of people around the globe. The focus of the TM organization has been to bring peace and enlightenment to all of the people of the world, by giving them an easy and systematic way to experience pure consciousness.

This experience of pure consciousness is not limited to any particular ethnic group, class, or caste. All you need is a functioning human nervous system. Bahá'u'lláh wrote, "He hath endowed every soul with the capacity to recognize the signs of God."[18]

In this brief overview, we have seen how the TM program is natural, practical, and beneficial. It can be verified through personal experience, scientific validation, and the ancient wisdom of the Vedic tradition. Finally, it is universal, available to everyone. Each of these criteria for validation is upheld in the Bahá'í writings.

Free to Choose

Before moving on, it may help to mention at this juncture that the Bahá'í Faith does not specify or endorse any particular procedure for meditation. Just because the TM program can be seen as a valid or even useful meditation technique according to Bahá'u'lláh's guidance for discerning truth, this does not mean that it is, or may some day become, recommended by any Bahá'í organization or institution. To do so would limit the freedom of each Bahá'í to choose, which was clearly upheld by the Guardian of the Faith, Shoghi Effendi, in one of his letters:

> He thinks it would be wiser for the Bahá'ís to use the Meditations given by Bahá'u'lláh, and not any set form of meditation recommended by someone else; but the believers must be left free in these details and allowed to have personal latitude in finding their own level of communion with God.[19]

Here we see the Guardian acknowledging the importance of free choice on the subject of meditation, even over his own opinion. The wisdom of this guidance has shaped my approach to how I discuss the TM program with friends and acquaintances, particularly since leaving MIU. Understanding that this is a personal matter, I rarely talk of meditation unless the subject comes up. When asked, I say that I practice the TM technique, and that it works well for me. Should anyone earnestly enquire further, I refer them to the TM organization for more information.

However, this approach leaves me feeling that I am not doing justice to this gift that I have been given. Is someone truly free to choose when they have limited understanding of the options? Although my knowledge of both the TM program and the Bahá'í Faith is far from perfect, I can at least recognize certain aspects of the TM program which a Bahá'í might be particularly concerned about, while I am also familiar with several Bahá'í teachings that someone practicing the TM program might be interested to know.

Thus, one goal in writing this book is to share what I think may be helpful for people in one these camps to reach a deeper level of understanding, if not appreciation, for what is available in the other. If I were to make any recommendation, it would be this: keep an open mind, investigate the truth for yourself, and if you choose any form of meditation, choose wisely.

With these thoughts in mind, let us next consider origins. Where does the TM program come from, exactly?

Notes

1. Bahá'u'lláh, *The Summons of the Lord of Hosts*, p 199

2. Bahá'u'lláh, "Tablet of Ahmad," *Bahá'í Prayers*, p 209

3. 'Abdu'l-Bahá, *Some Answered Questions*, pp 8,9

4. Bahá'u'lláh, *Tablets of Bahá'u'lláh*, p 142

5. Shoghi Effendi, quoted in the compilation *Prayer and Devotional Life*, #50

6. Bahá'u'lláh, *Gleanings from the Writings of Bahá'u'lláh*, LXXVII

7. Bahá'u'lláh, *Tablets of Bahá'u'lláh*, p 171

8. Ibid, p 138

9. Ibid, p 157

10. Bahá'u'lláh, *The Call of the Divine Beloved*, p 88

11. 'Abdu'l-Bahá, *The Promulgation of Universal Peace*, p 291

12. 'Abdu'l-Bahá, *Paris Talks*, p 146

13. Ibid, p 137

14. Shoghi Effendi, quoted in the compilation *Prayer and Devotional Life*, #46

15. Maharishi Mahesh Yogi, "Celebrating 12 January 2008." *Global Good News*, p 2

16. Bahá'u'lláh, *Tablets of Bahá'u'lláh*, p 144

17. Bahá'u'lláh, *Gleanings from the Writings of Bahá'u'lláh*, XLIII

18. Ibid, LII

19. From a letter dated 27 January 1952 written on behalf of Shoghi Effendi to an individual believer, *Prayer and Devotional Life*, The Role of Meditation, Extract 47

Origins

Ever since learning TM, an important question for me has been: Where does it come from? What is the origin? This was one of my motivations for enrolling in MIU and for choosing to major in Natural Law. In the first few weeks at MIU I realized that Bahá'u'lláh must be the Return of Christ, and that His Revelation stirred the whole creation to its very depths. The next logical question for me was: Could it be that this Revelation is somehow connected to the origins of the TM program? I spent the better part of eight years pondering answers to that and related questions. Here are some of the avenues I explored.

The Vedas

Maharishi teaches that the Vedas are far more than ancient writings of some lost civilization. The Vedas, he says, are the blueprint of creation, embedded into the creation, and available to each one of us in the simplest form of our own awareness. They are the song of life, the song of the Self, to itSelf, by itSelf. The Vedas are structured in consciousness, in pure consciousness. Those whose awareness is open to pure consciousness are able to experience the Vedas in their true form.

There are some who not only experience the Vedas, but can perceive impulses of creative intelligence lively within them. These impulses are vibrations within the Unified Field of Natural Law, that are perceived as sounds. These sounds join into melodies and hymns with meaningful words. The words are seen, or cognized, in written characters in the Devanagari script, or Sanskrit, the language of the Vedas. Someone who cognizes the Vedas is called a "Rishi", or "Seer". The Vedic literature is a collection of cognitions from rishis of past centuries and ages.

Revival

This understanding of the Vedas is fairly recent. Maharishi credits his teacher, Guru Dev, for bringing these simple but profound concepts to light, and he has then followed up by offering them to the world. When asked "why now", why has this ancient knowledge that was lost for so long only now being made available, Maharishi responds: "It is the need of the times."

Truly, we are living in a time like no other. Never before have we seen so many people turn away from traditional religion while at the same time express such a thirst for spiritual knowledge. And never before could a holy man of India hop on a jet plane to the West, share this message on television, record lectures on videotape, and train thousands of teachers around the world. There is a perfect combination of motive, means, and opportunity for a revival of Vedic knowledge in the very time that we are living.

The Vedic Tradition talks about four ages, or "yugas". They are Sat Yuga, Krita Yuga, Treta Yuga, and Kali Yuga. Maharishi says that these four yugas are characterized by the level of natural law being lived by the people in their daily lives. During Sat Yuga, people lived at a very high level of natural law. They were honest, trustworthy, and embodied all good qualities. But people eventually got more interested in superficial aspects of reality, and neglected to maintain a close connection to pure consciousness, the source of natural law. So the pure civilization declined a little. In each subsequent age, this connection to pure consciousness, the home of all of the laws of nature, diminished more and more, until eventually the world entered Kali Yuga, where evil is everywhere and people are miserable. That's pretty much where we are today.

But then, suddenly, there is a great leap. It is not a gradual change, but a great leap—from Kali Yuga back to Sat Yuga. What causes that leap? As Maharishi says, it is the "need of the times." And he says this is what we are experiencing right now. This leap back to Sat Yuga, back to 100% of natural law being lived in the lives of the people, is in some ways the cause and in other ways the effect of Maharishi's revival of Vedic knowledge. On the personal level, people will enjoy a life of bliss and fulfillment, and on the collective level we will have world peace and invincibility for all nations.

This concept of the great leap back to 100% of natural law lived in people's lives is mentioned by Lord Krishna in the *Bhagavad-Gita*, which Maharishi calls the "Scripture of the Vedas." Krishna explains that when goodness ("dharma") is fading away and evil ("adharma") seems to be taking over, then He appears to save humanity. He said, "Whenever dharma is in decay, and adharma flourishes, Oh Bharata, then I create Myself to protect the righteous and destroy the wicked, to establish dharma firmly, I take birth age after age."[1]

This quote is taken from a translation and commentary on the *Bhagavad-Gita* written by Maharishi. In the commentary on this verse, Maharishi says, "The establishment of dharma in God's creation is His own work. He does it. He does it again and again, either through the automatic arrangement of His government, He Himself remaining behind the scenes, or by taking a body and coming to be active in the affairs of the world."[2]

This type of re-creation, of rebirth, is not unique to the *Bhagavad-Gita*. It is expressed in the scriptures of all religions. Buddha said, "I am not the first Buddha who came upon the earth, nor shall I be the last... In due time another Buddha will arise."[3] Moses said, "The Lord your God will raise up for you a prophet like me from among you, from your brethren—him you shall heed—"[4] Jesus said, "... and they will see the Son of man coming on the clouds of heaven with power and great glory;"[5] Muḥammad said that every group of people receives a prophet like Himself, acting as both a comforter and a warner: "Verily we have sent thee with the truth; a bearer of good tidings and a warner; nor hath there been a people unvisited by its warner."[6]

Bahá'u'lláh affirms this idea of the return of God's Messenger at the end of one age, to inaugurate a new age:

And now concerning thy question regarding the nature of religion. Know thou that they who are truly wise have likened the world unto the human temple. As the body of man needeth a garment to clothe it, so the body of mankind must needs be adorned with the mantle of justice and wisdom. Its robe is the Revelation vouchsafed unto it by God. Whenever this robe hath fulfilled its purpose, the Almighty will assuredly renew it. For every age requireth a fresh measure of the light of God. Every Divine Revelation hath been sent down in a manner that befitted the circumstances of the age in which it hath appeared.[7]

Divine Teacher

Each of these Messengers of God is a divine teacher. Each guides humanity to grow and develop. Maharishi tells us that Krishna gave to humanity the wisdom of the Vedas in ancient times, but over time it was lost:

The Blessed Lord said: I proclaimed this imperishable Yoga to Vivasvat, Vivasvat declared it to Manu and Manu to Ikshavaku. Thus having received it one from another, the royal sages knew it. With the long lapse of time, O scorcher of enemies, this Yoga has been lost to the world.[8]

The theme of the *Bhagavad-Gita*, according to Maharishi, is Krishna reviving once again the timeless truths of life, which he calls Yoga. Maharishi comments:

The Yoga expounded by Lord Krishna is imperishable because it brings to light the wisdom of the Absolute and the wisdom of the relative. The relative and the Absolute, both these are eternal; and so is Yoga, which expounds the truth of both, the truth of life in its fullness. It is eternal because it serves the cosmic purpose and it is natural to the mind of man.[9]

Thus we see that Maharishi attributes the ultimate origin of this ancient wisdom to Krishna. When He takes birth, age after age, He imparts this knowledge to humanity.

This concept of a divine Messenger as the original source of ancient knowledge is affirmed in the Bahá'í writings. Bahá'u'lláh said, "The sages aforetime acquired their knowledge from the Prophets, inasmuch as the latter were the Exponents of divine philosophy and the Revealers of heavenly mysteries."[10] This passage is found in the Tablet of Wisdom (Lawḥ-i-Ḥikmat) revealed by Bahá'u'lláh in answer to questions related to philosophy posed by Áqá Muḥammad, an early Bahá'í. The tablet goes on to give examples of how the various philosophers gained knowledge from Prophets of God.

At the end of this exposition, Bahá'u'lláh reiterates the respect and reverence that the wise have towards God, as well as the blessings that God bestows upon them.

> A true philosopher would never deny God nor His evidences, rather would he acknowledge His glory and overpowering majesty which overshadow all created things. Verily We love those men of knowledge who have brought to light such things as promote the best interests of humanity, and We aided them through the potency of Our behest, for well are We able to achieve Our purpose.[11]

Clearly there is a link, validated by both Maharishi and Bahá'u'lláh, between God's Messengers and the philosophers and sages of ancient times. It is a relationship of Teacher to learner, of Giver to recipient. Could not this also be true today? Could the Great Leap, the revival of the ancient wisdom of the Vedas by Guru Dev and Maharishi be related somehow to the birth of a new revelation from God, the Bahá'í Revelation? Could there be a connection?

Revelation

The Bahá'í Revelation is staggering. It is so totally all-encompassing that it almost defies description or explanation. To give you some perspective of its scope, consider that the advent of Bahá'u'lláh fulfills the expectations of all the world's major religions.

Shoghi Effendi, the Guardian of the Bahá'í Faith tells us, "To Israel He (Bahá'u'lláh) was neither more nor less than the incarnation of the 'Everlasting Father,' the 'Lord of Hosts' come down 'with ten thousands of saints'; to Christendom Christ returned 'in the glory of the Father'; to Shí'ih Islám the return of the Imám Husayn; to Sunní Islám the descent of the 'Spirit of God' (Jesus Christ); to the Zoroastrians the promised Sháh-Bahrám; to the Hindus the reincarnation of Krishna; to the Buddhists the fifth Buddha."[12]

This Revelation is actually a twin revelation, revealed by two successive Manifestations of God, the Báb, and Bahá'u'lláh, born just two years apart. The Báb was the Forerunner of Bahá'u'lláh, announcing His Mission in much the same way as John the Baptist announced the coming of Jesus. And yet the Báb was also an independent Manifestation of God, the Founder of an independent religion. The revelations of the Báb and Bahá'u'lláh are closely linked, and together make up the Bahá'í Revelation. The Báb often referred to Bahá'u'lláh in his writings, and Bahá'u'lláh often referred to the Báb as well. In this sense, Bahá'u'lláh once wrote:

> No understanding can grasp the nature of His Revelation, nor can any knowledge comprehend the full measure of His Faith. All sayings are dependent upon His sanction, and all things stand in need of His Cause. All else save Him are created by His command, and move and have their being through His law. He is the Revealer of the divine mysteries, and the Expounder of the hidden and ancient wisdom.[13]

The power and scope of the Bahá'í Revelation is beyond human imagination. Bahá'u'lláh said:

> Say: It is in Our power, should We wish it, to cause all created things to expire in an instant, and, with the next, to endue them again with life. The knowledge thereof, however, is with God alone, the All-Knowing, the All-Informed. It is in Our power, should We wish it, to enable a speck of floating dust to generate, in less than the twinkling of an eye, suns of infinite, of unimaginable splendour, to cause a dewdrop to develop into vast and numberless oceans, to infuse into every letter such a force as to empower it to unfold all the knowledge of past and future ages. This, in truth, is a matter simple of accomplishment. Such have been the evidences of My power from the beginning that hath no beginning until the end that hath no end. My creatures, however,

have been oblivious of My power, have repudiated My sovereignty, and contended with Mine own Self, the All-Knowing, the All-Wise.[14]

We mere mortals, we creatures, are for the most part oblivious of this incredible power. We go about our daily lives, doing our work, enjoying the love of our families, rarely contemplating God's power, perhaps even questioning His existence—or the relevance of religion. In reality, though, we are all completely dependent upon God. Bahá'u'lláh said:

Of all that lieth between heaven and earth, naught can stir except by My leave, and unto My Kingdom none can ascend save at My behest. My creatures, however, have remained veiled from My might and My sovereignty, and are numbered with the heedless.[15]

He likens us to leaves, attached to a tree. We sprout from the tree, and are nourished by its sap. It is through Him that we have life. Plucked from the tree, we would soon die. He said:

My creatures are even as the leaves of a tree. They proceed from the tree, and depend upon it for their existence, yet remain oblivious of their root and origin. We draw such similitudes for the sake of Our discerning servants that perchance they may transcend a mere plant-like level of existence and attain unto true maturity in this resistless and immovable Cause.[16]

The time has come for humanity to reach a level of maturity unknown in previous ages. This is our true station, our promised destiny. We must and we shall reach our full potential in this new age.

> The potentialities inherent in the station of man, the full measure of his destiny on earth, the innate excellence of his reality, must all be manifested in this promised Day of God.[17] - Bahá'u'lláh.

Among the miracles of this Day of God is the power of His Revelation to transform humanity, through the Word of God. Bahá'u'lláh said:

> Every word that proceedeth out of the mouth of God is endowed with such potency as can instill new life into every human frame, if ye be of them that comprehend this truth. All the wondrous works ye behold in this world have been manifested through the operation of His supreme and most exalted Will, His wondrous and inflexible Purpose.[18]

The Word of God has a transformative power that permeates the entire creation, reaching the minds and hearts of humanity and instilling new capacities into every soul. He continues:

> Through the mere revelation of the word "Fashioner," issuing forth from His lips and proclaiming His attribute to mankind, such power is released as can generate, through successive ages, all the manifold arts which the hands of man can produce. ... In like manner,

the moment the word expressing My attribute "The Omniscient" issueth forth from My mouth, every created thing will, according to its capacity and limitations, be invested with the power to unfold the knowledge of the most marvelous sciences, and will be empowered to manifest them in the course of time at the bidding of Him Who is the Almighty, the All-Knowing.[19]

Since the first announcement of this Revelation in 1844, the world has seen more advances in the arts, sciences, and technologies than in all previously recorded history, and the pace of new discoveries and inventions increases exponentially. Consider communications. Starting with the first telegraph message in that same year of 1844, we then saw the telephone, phonograph, radio, and television, and more recently email, the world wide web, and smart phone technology. Or transportation, where we've taken to the skies and now circle the globe and even travel to the moon and beyond. The pace of scientific discovery continues to increase as human knowledge doubles in days, or even hours.

Underlying these technologies are the pure sciences. Physicists have transformed our perceptions of the world with their theories of general relativity and quantum mechanics. Biologists probe deeply into DNA, the blueprint of life, and the human genome. Huge advances are being made in chemistry, geology, and the earth sciences, while new disciplines of psychology, social sciences, economics and environmental studies expand our horizons.

But hold on, you might say. What is the connection to the Bahá'í Revelation? After all, Albert Einstein, Max Planck, Watson, Crick and all of the rest of today's top scientists came long after Bahá'u'lláh. Few if any were exposed to His teachings, or had ever even heard of Him.

Nevertheless, all of us, from the most humble to the most learned, have been influenced through the power of this Revelation. Bahá'u'lláh said:

> Through the movement of Our Pen of glory We have, at the bidding of the omnipotent Ordainer, breathed a new life into every human frame, and instilled into every word a fresh potency. All created things proclaim the evidences of this worldwide regeneration.[20]

Of all of the various sciences and technologies that have been discovered and developed in this new age, amazing as they are, few compare to Maharishi Vedic Science and the related technology of the Unified Field. Like the founders of modern physics and organic chemistry, Maharishi also lived decades after the passing of Bahá'u'lláh. Even Maharishi's teacher, Guru Dev, to whom he attributes this re-awakening of the Vedic knowledge, was born in 1871, many years after the declaration of the Báb in 1844 that inaugurated this Revelation. And yet both of them come under its influence. In fact, Bahá'u'lláh foretold that the greater the capacity of the individual, the greater will be his or her power to unfold the knowledge of the sciences. He said:

> ...every created thing will, according to its capacity and limitations, be invested with the power to unfold the knowledge of the most marvelous sciences, and will be empowered to manifest them in the course of time at the bidding of Him Who is the Almighty, the All-Knowing.[21]

All of this takes place over the course of time, and is at God's bidding. For this reason I feel reassured in my understanding that the "need of the times" and the "Great Leap" that bring this knowledge of the Vedas to light point to the Revelation of Bahá'u'lláh.

All Knowledge

One of the most exciting and overwhelming aspects of the teachings of both Bahá'u'lláh and Maharishi is the concept of all knowledge. When I was in high school my friend once said to me, "Just think, Bob, how much more there is to learn. Humanity only knows 1% of everything there is to know." I had to chuckle at the naivety of such a statement. How can you calculate that 1% unless you know the other 99% to make the comparison, I wondered.

Bahá'u'lláh quotes a tradition known to Muslim clerics and scholars that says:

Knowledge is twenty and seven letters. All that the Prophets have revealed are two letters thereof. No man thus far hath known more than these two letters. But when the Qá'im shall arise, He will cause the remaining twenty and five letters to be made manifest.[22]

The "Qá'im" is the Promised One in S̲h̲í'ih Islám. The Báb claimed to fulfill the prophecies concerning the Qá'im, and this claim was upheld by Bahá'u'lláh. One of these prophecies was this one, concerning all knowledge. Like many passages of scripture, this should not be taken literally. The twenty-seven letters mentioned are not literal letters of the alphabet like A, B, and C. They represent something deeper, something more abstract. The point here is that however you consider knowledge to be, before now humanity had limited access to it, and since the Revelation of the Báb, the totality of knowledge is now available. Bahá'u'lláh continues:

Consider, He hath declared Knowledge to consist of twenty and seven letters, and regarded all the Prophets, from Adam even unto the 'Seal,' (Muḥammad) as Expounders of only two letters thereof and of having been sent down with these two letters. He also saith that the Qá'im will reveal all the remaining twenty and five letters.[23]

Since the Qá'im (the Báb) has come, and His Revelation is manifest, we now have access to all knowledge. So it should not come as a surprise that Maharishi talks about having access to all knowledge. Pure consciousness, he says, is the home of all knowledge. "If one's conscious mind is open to the field of pure consciousness, the home of all knowledge is structured on the level of one's awareness,"[24] he said.

It's a little like being able to hold a seed in your hand. That seed gives you the DNA, which in a way is the essence, the potential, of the whole tree. Wrapped up in pure consciousness you have all the laws of nature. It is the Unified Field of Natural Law. As you grow in your experience of higher states of consciousness, this Unified Field becomes more and more lively in your own awareness. Maharishi said, "The unified field is the field of all knowledge in seed form."[25]

Concealment

There is one more thing to consider regarding this Revelation. Although it is truly magnificent and all-encompassing, yet it is also difficult to recognize and appreciate. People caught up in the superficial things of life, who cling to their own ideas of who God is and how He operates, who hold tightly to literal translations of scripture, or who refuse to investigate truth for themselves, these people may miss it altogether. Referring to them, Bahá'u'lláh wrote:

> ...such a Revelation these mean and depraved people have sought to measure with their own deficient minds, their own deficient learning and understanding. Should

it fail to conform to their standards, they straightway reject it.[26]

Going even beyond this, Bahá'u'lláh says that even the most knowledgeable, the pure and devoted souls, and even God's own Prophets may not be aware of this Revelation. Or, it is possible that they know, but don't have permission to tell. He says:

A Revelation, of which the Prophets of God, His saints and chosen ones, have either not been informed, or which, in pursuance of God's inscrutable Decree, they have not disclosed...[27]

Why would this be? Why would this be kept secret? I'm not completely sure, but this passage from the Writings of Bahá'u'lláh suggests an answer:

Say: If it be Our pleasure We shall render the Cause victorious through the power of a single word from Our presence. He is in truth the Omnipotent, the All-Compelling. Should it be God's intention, there would appear out of the forests of celestial might the lion of indomitable strength whose roaring is like unto the peals of thunder reverberating in the mountains....[28]

Surely it is in God's power to proclaim the Revelation in such a way that nobody could deny it. But that is not what is happening. He continues:

... However, since Our loving providence surpasseth all things, We have ordained that complete victory should be achieved through speech and utterance, that Our servants throughout the earth may thereby become the recipients of divine good. This is but a token of God's bounty vouchsafed unto them. Verily thy Lord is the All-Sufficing, the Most Exalted.[29]

Bahá'u'lláh has given the task of teaching His Cause, of proclaiming His Revelation, to His servants. They need to speak out His Message, and even more challenging, they need to live it. Only when people see the transformation of character in its followers that the Faith brings about will they believe that such a Revelation has taken place.

Another reason for concealing the Revelation is to test us. Bahá'u'lláh makes it clear that God's way is to test His servants, so that their true nature comes to light. He said, "Reflect upon the strange and manifold trials with which He doth test His servants."[30]

These tests are for our benefit, so that we will find God through our own efforts and will-power. In this Revelation we cannot rely on anyone else. We cannot hold a clergyman responsible for our faith, or our mothers or fathers. We cannot fall back on the endorsement of celebrities, sports heroes, or 4 out of 5 doctors. On the subject of faith, we cannot evade responsibility by placing the decision into the hands of a sage or guru, no matter how enlightened. Bahá'u'lláh wrote, "For the faith of no man can be conditioned by anyone except himself."[31]

For these three reasons—so that each one of us should face our tests, should have opportunities to teach, and should take responsibility for our own spiritual development, I believe that Maharishi may have been guided (or known intuitively) not to talk about the Bahá'í Revelation. It is difficult for me to imagine that he did not know about it, but perhaps in "pursuance of God's inscrutable Decree" he did not directly disclose it.

What might have happened otherwise? Most likely confusion would have arisen among practitioners of TM, as well as among the Bahá'ís. By keeping his Vedic revival almost entirely separate from discussions about God and religion, by couching it in terms of science, it could appeal to people from any religion, or no religion. Bahá'ís worldwide are familiar with the confusion and conflicts over religion prevalent in today's society. Rather than getting involved in all of that, Maharishi has presented the wisdom of the Vedas in almost completely non-religious terms and concepts.

As we have seen, it is possible to find connections between the Bahá'í Revelation and Maharishi's revival of the Vedas. These are not obvious, but with a little bit of understanding and a small measure of faith, we can bring them to light.

Notes

1. Maharishi Mahesh Yogi, *Bhagavad-Gita - A New Translation and Commentary*, pp 190,191

2. Ibid, p 192

3. Buddha, *The Gospel Of Buddha*, XCVI:13

4. *The Bible*, Revised Standard Version, Deuteronomy 18:15

5. Ibid, Matthew 24:30

6. *The Koran* Súrih 35, verse 24

7. Bahá'u'lláh, *Gleanings from the Writings of Bahá'u'lláh*, XXXIV

8. *Bhagavad-Gita - A New Translation and Commentary* 4:1-2

9. Maharishi Mahesh Yogi, *Bhagavad-Gita - A New Translation and Commentary*, p 183

10. Bahá'u'lláh, *Tablets of Bahá'u'lláh*, pp 144-145

11. Ibid, p 150

12. Shoghi Effendi, *God Passes By*, p 94

13. Bahá'u'lláh, *Kitáb-i-Iqán (The Book of Certitude)*, p 243

14. Bahá'u'lláh, *The Summons of the Lord of Hosts*, p 75

15. Ibid, p 40

16. Ibid

17. Bahá'u'lláh, *Gleanings from the Writings of Bahá'u'lláh*, CLXII

18. Ibid, LXXIV

19. Ibid, LXXIV

20. Ibid, XLIII

21. Ibid, LXXIV

22. Bahá'u'lláh, *Kitáb-i-Íqán (The Book of Certitude)*, p 243

23. Ibid, pp 243-244

24. Maharishi Mahesh Yogi, quoted in "The Maharishi Technology of the Unified Field in Education: Principles, Practice, and Research.", p 4

25. Ibid, p 6

26. Bahá'u'lláh, *Kitáb-i-Íqán (The Book of Certitude)*, p 244

27. Ibid

28. Bahá'u'lláh, *Tablets of Bahá'u'lláh*, p 197

29. Ibid, pp 197-198

30. Bahá'u'lláh, *Kitáb-i-Íqán (The Book of Certitude)*, p 55

31. Bahá'u'lláh, *Gleanings from the Writings of Bahá'u'lláh*, LXXV

Harmony

So far we have used the Bahá'í writings to evaluate the TM program and some of Maharishi's teachings and claims, and we've looked at how these two significant initiatives may have deep connections that are not obvious at first glance. Now perhaps we can consider prospects for harmony between the TM program and the Bahá'í Faith.

Purpose

"You don't need Transcendental Meditation to be a good Bahá'í." The words caught me by surprise and left me a bit disheartened. They were delivered in a talk by a well-known and highly respected member of the Bahá'í community a few years ago. The subject was Spirituality and the Bahá'í Faith, and he was explaining the power of the Creative Word of Bahá'u'lláh for personal transformation. Although I feel what he said is not incorrect, I found his choice of words ill-considered.

Suppose he had said, "You don't need a computer to be a good Bahá'í," or "You don't need to be healthy to be a good Bahá'í." Both of these statements are also true. So, does that mean Bahá'ís shouldn't use computers or take care of their health?

Sure, a person may not need a computer to be a good Bahá'í. But they might find it useful for doing Bahá'í work like administrative tasks, communications, and researching the writings. Applied to these and similar tasks, computers can play a role in unifying humanity. The Guardian may have foreseen computing technology back in 1936 when he wrote, "A mechanism of world inter-communication will be devised, embracing the whole planet, freed from national hindrances and restrictions, and functioning with marvellous swiftness and perfect regularity."[1] The Revelation of Bahá'u'lláh has unlocked human potential, allowing us to make new discoveries and develop new technologies like computers. For a Bahá'í, the purpose of life is to know and to worship God, and to carry forward an ever-advancing civilization. To whatever extent technology can assist, should it not be used as a means to this end?

In a similar way, good health in itself will not make someone a better Bahá'í, but it may provide more opportunities. When we are healthy we can do more. 'Abdu'l-Bahá said, "The bounty of good health is the greatest of all gifts."[2] And what is the purpose of such a gift?

During my time at MIU, Maharishi was developing courses in Ayurveda, the part of the Vedas related to life and health. He sent some Ayurvedic doctors and pundits from India to Iowa to introduce some of the basic concepts to us. In a large lecture hall filled with MIU students and faculty, they presented the Ayurvedic knowledge to develop perfect health in the direction of immortality. They concluded their lecture with these words, "And of course, what is the purpose of good health? To serve God!" A palpable wave of surprise and bemusement passed through the room. This conclusion, so self-evident to the pundits, astonished the audience, who were not used to hearing the word "God" in this context.

What makes someone a good Bahá'í is not what they may have, but how they use it. It seems to me that to accept God's gifts and use them in His service is what any aspiring Bahá'í would strive to do. "How shall we utilize these gifts and expend these bounties? By directing our efforts toward the unification of the human race..."[3] is how 'Abdu'l-Bahá said it. In like manner, if we understand TM as a gift to help us develop our minds, improve our health, to reduce anxiety and stress, and to reach our full human potential, why should we not accept it? Why not apply it to improve ourselves to become better servants to humanity and to God?

In a talk given in New York City, 'Abdu'l-Bahá said, "We must make the soil of our hearts receptive and fertile by tilling in order that the rain of divine mercy may refresh them and bring forth roses and hyacinths of heavenly planting."[4] As I see it, the role of TM is to till the soil of our hearts, so that it is more receptive. Then we choose carefully what to plant there. If we plant weeds, they will become healthy weeds. But if we plant roses and hyacinths, we will have abundant beauty and fragrance. TM does not dictate what gets planted in our hearts. That is up to us. But it does help us cultivate the soil.

'Abdu'l-Bahá also used an analogy of a mirror to explain how we develop our spiritual nature. He said the mirror can reflect the sun, but it needs two things. It must be cleaned, and it must be turned towards the sun. "...when the mirror is polished and turned towards the sun it should manifest the rays thereof."[5]

Like tilling the soil, this analogy offers a way to understand the relationship between TM and the Bahá'í Faith. There are two actions here: polishing the mirror, and turning it towards the sun. You can polish the mirror until it is bright and shiny, but if you keep it pointed to the ground, it will reflect the ground. On the other hand, if the mirror is covered with dust or tarnish, pointing it towards the sun won't have much effect. It will not reflect the light very well.

In my experience, doing TM is like polishing the mirror. Every day, morning and evening, you allow your mind to bathe itself in the experience of pure consciousness, and you come out feeling rested, refreshed and uplifted. At that point you have a choice. You decide what to do with your clean, refreshed mind and body. You can direct the mirror of your heart towards God, the Source of life, or you can turn away. Making this choice is where, for me, the Bahá'í teachings and writings come into play. Every morning, for example, I first meditate, then pray. Then I go about my daily life, with family and friends, work, study, and recreation, following to the best of my ability the teachings of the Bahá'í Faith. Do I need TM to be a good Bahá'í? Perhaps not, but through God's mercy and grace, it has helped me to become that better person that God wants me to be.

Conflict or Compatible?

In his book, *When Science Meets Religion*, Ian G. Barbour identifies four views of science and religion, four ways that he has seen them interact: Conflict, Independence, Dialog, and Integration. Although his focus is on Western science and its relationship with Christianity, perhaps these viewpoints can be helpful when considering prospects for harmony between TM and the Bahá'í Faith.

Among all the people with whom I've had a chance to discuss the relationship between TM and the Bahá'í Faith, it seems there are valid reasons for adopting any of these four viewpoints. There are ways in which these two appear to be in Conflict, at least on the surface. Getting past these superficial differences, many people are content to keep each system of knowledge Independent, and typically focus on just one of them. On the other hand, there are people who are somewhat involved in both, such as myself and other Bahá'ís I knew at MIU. We often found ourselves in Dialog between these two vast bodies of knowledge. That dialog may lead, ultimately, to attempting Integration in some way.

Perhaps it is possible to gather the viewpoints of Independence, Dialog, and Integration into a broad category of Compatibility. The question then gets simplified into whether TM and the Bahá'í Faith are in conflict, or are they in any way compatible?

Personally, I think they are compatible, but not everyone sees it that way. After all, if someone wants to find conflict between the teachings of Maharishi and the Bahá'í Faith, they can, and they may not be willing to consider other points of view. It is not my intent to argue or try to convince them. But others may have sincere questions, which deserve reasonable responses. Three topics come immediately to mind that raise questions about compatibility: the concept of suffering, the belief in reincarnation, and the fear of God. There may be others, but these will suffice as examples to show how perceived conflicts may turn out to be simply in the eye of the beholder.

The Concept of Suffering

"Life is not suffering. Life is bliss." How many times has Maharishi said that? It is not our destiny to suffer. Enlightenment is our birthright, he used to say. Perhaps he was speaking to the Protestant ethic, humorously summed up by my brother, Bill, as "Work, suffer, and die." Suffering is certainly prominent in Christianity, and also plays a significant role in spiritual growth, according to Bahá'í teachings. 'Abdu'l-Bahá said, "To attain eternal happiness one must suffer."[6]

Comparing the statements of Maharishi and 'Abdu'l-Bahá, it's easy to see how someone might think that the two paths are in conflict, seemingly diametrically opposed. One says that life is not suffering, the other that suffering is necessary for happiness.

If we look deeper, though, we might arrive at a different conclusion. First of all, neither Maharishi nor 'Abdu'l-Bahá denies the existence of suffering. And I believe that neither would wish suffering on anyone. Both of them devoted their lives to alleviate the sufferings of others.

Perhaps the clue to reconciliation of viewpoints comes in this subsequent statement spoken by 'Abdu'l-Bahá: "He who has reached the state of self-sacrifice has true joy."[7] Here he links suffering to the concept of sacrifice. Any suffering we may experience during our lifetime may be seen as having a higher purpose, a spiritual purpose, which leads to far greater joy.

Maharishi often told the story of a man living in a small, miserable hut, who is given the opportunity to move into a beautiful palace. On the one hand, he is excited about the chance to improve his lot, but on the other hand, he hasn't seen it yet, and so he mourns the loss of his hut. "Oh, my poor hut," he says.

This story points to the deeper meaning of suffering, as I understand it. The deepest suffering must be due to separation from God, from living out of tune with natural law, as it were. On other levels, suffering may result from the temporary stresses associated with changing our habits to adopt a new lifestyle, a new mentality. We are living in the hut, metaphorically separate from God (the palace owner), and so we suffer deeply. That is not true life. True life is freedom from that suffering. But unless life in the hut is unpleasant, we won't want to move at all. We will just stay stuck there. Imagine, despite all the promises of the palace, many prefer to hedge their bets and stay in the hut. Maybe they have found a dry corner, with fewer leaks in the roof. Or maybe they don't believe there is a palace, or that it is any better. Their love of the hut keeps them there, like a prisoner. "Free thyself from the fetters of this world, and loose thy soul from the prison of self. Seize thy chance, for it will come to thee no more,"[8] said Bahá'u'lláh.

Those who suffer most in the hut are the most eager to leave it. That's why suffering is necessary. "The steed of this valley is pain, and if there be no pain this journey will never end,"[9] said Bahá'u'lláh. The life without suffering, without pain, the life of bliss that Maharishi is talking about is a spiritual life, an enlightened life, a life lived in tune with natural law. That life is not suffering. That life is bliss. And that life is the life that suffering points us towards. Most of us need a certain measure of suffering to push us toward that greater happiness, that nearness to God. From this point of view, the teachings of Maharishi and the Bahá'í Faith on suffering can be seen as compatible.

Reincarnation

Among many of the TM meditators I have met, there is tacit acceptance of the idea of reincarnation. Although sometimes vaguely defined, or referred to in a joking way, the general notion is that we go through cycles of birth and death in this world, working our way towards higher states of consciousness, until we finally achieve liberation, Unity Consciousness, or Brahman.

I cannot remember hearing Maharishi talk on this subject in any audio or video tape, but there are passages in the *Bhagavad-Gita* that are often used to support this point of view. For example, at one point Krishna says to Arjuna, "Many births have passed for Me and for you also, O Arjuna. I know them all, but you know them not, O scorcher of enemies."[10]

The Bahá'í teachings do not support the idea of reincarnation. 'Abdu'l-Bahá discussed it at length in a chapter of the book *Some Answered Questions*. One point he raised is that "return" as mentioned in scripture is of the qualities and attributes of a person, and not their individuality. He also explained how the return of imperfection will not bring about perfection. He said that we move upwards through all of the levels of existence, not back and forth:

By God's eternal grace the true capacity and receptivity of the human reality is made clear and manifest through traversing the degrees of existence and not through recurrence and return. When the shell is opened but once, it is made plain and clear whether it conceals a shining pearl or worthless matter. ... Apart from this, advancing and moving through the worlds in a direct line and according to the natural order is the cause of existence, and moving against the natural order and arrangement of things is the cause of extinction. The return of the spirit after death is incompatible with the natural movement and contrary to the divine order.[11]

So how do we reconcile these teachings with what it says in the *Bhagavad-Gita*? I believe it is possible. For one thing, there is much commonality on the level of principle. If we look more closely at what the *Bhagavad-Gita* says, we can find parallel truths in the Bahá'í writings. For example, both agree that the physical human body is not permanent:

"These bodies are known to have an end;"[12] - Krishna

"These material bodies are composed of atoms; when these atoms begin to separate decomposition sets in, then comes what we call death. This composition of atoms, which constitutes the body or mortal element of any created being, is temporary."[13] - 'Abdu'l-Bahá

In contrast, the soul is permanent:

"... the dweller in the body is eternal, imperishable, infinite..."[14] - Krishna

"With the soul it is different. The soul is not a combination of elements, it is not composed of many atoms, it is of one indivisible substance and therefore eternal."[15] - 'Abdu'l-Bahá

This idea of the unity and permanence of the soul versus the composite and temporary nature of the body is expressed this way by Maharishi, in his commentary on the *Bhagavad-Gita*: "Reality is one, omnipresent, devoid of any duality, without components—that is why it cannot be slain. The body is composed of different parts—that is why it can be slain."[16]

The next point of agreement is that although the physical body will die, there will be a rebirth:

"Certain indeed is death for the born and certain is birth for the dead; therefore over the inevitable you should not grieve."[17] - Krishna

"O son, if thou art able not to sleep, then thou art able not to die. And if thou art able not to waken after sleep, then thou shalt be able not to rise after death."[18] - Bahá'u'lláh

The soul will be reborn, in a new way:

"As a man casting off worn-out garments, takes other new ones, so the dweller in the body casting off worn-out bodies takes others that are new."[19] - Krishna

"Know thou of a truth that the soul, after its separation from the body, will continue to progress until it attaineth the presence of God, in a state and condition which neither the revolution of ages and centuries, nor the changes and chances of this world, can alter.... The world beyond is as different from this world as this world is different from that of the child while still in the womb of its mother. When the soul attaineth the Presence of God, it will assume the form that best befitteth its immortality and is worthy of its celestial habitation."[20] - Bahá'u'lláh

We come from God, and to Him we will return:

"Creatures are unmanifest in the beginning, manifest in the middle state, and unmanifest again in the end, Oh Bharata! What grief is there in this?"[21] - Krishna

"The truth that shineth bright and resplendent as the sun is this, that all have been created through the operation of the Divine Will and have proceeded from the same source, that all are from Him and that unto Him they shall all return."[22] - Bahá'u'lláh

I find much in common among these passages. In fact, it seems that the only real point of difference between the Bahá'í teachings and the commonly-held understanding of the *Bhagavad-Gita* is the nature of the rebirth of the soul. This may be due to the interpretation of the words "birth" and "body" in the *Bhagavad-Gita*. Taken literally, they suggest physical birth back into this world in another physical body. Could there be a deeper interpretation?

In a later commentary on the idea of "many births"[23] Maharishi explains that during the experience of Transcendental Consciousness during meditation, a person, however briefly, becomes pure Existence, and is then reborn when returning to individuality. "Thus," he says, "there is absolutely no reason to suppose that the expression 'many births' means many lifetimes."[24]

Maharishi goes on to say that even a superficial interpretation of "many births" could be referring to those who stray from the practise of Yoga (or TM) and thus might only achieve enlightenment "through practise in many lives."[25] What does "many lives" mean in that context? Do people who don't achieve enlightenment in this physical world really need to come back here and keep trying until they get it right? Or can this also be understood in a deeper way?

The Bahá'í Revelation has expanded our understanding of spiritual reality, opening our awareness to the existence of many worlds of God beyond this physical world. It's not just two options anymore—heaven or hell. There are an infinite number of worlds into which we can and will be reborn. Our progress will be infinite. 'Abdu'l-Bahá said:

> ... certain reincarnationists imagine existence to be confined to this fleeting world, and deny the other worlds of God, whereas in reality the latter are infinite....

For in this universe of God's, which appears in the utmost perfection, beauty, and grandeur, the luminous bodies of the material universe are infinite. Pause to infer, then, how infinite and unbounded the spiritual realms of God, which are the very foundation, must be!"[26]

To me this suggests that all of us will be reborn, many times, but not here in this physical world. Those on the path of evolution, of growth towards God, will have opportunities to continue growing as they are reborn into those other, spiritual worlds. Bahá'u'lláh said:

O My servants! ... Worlds, holy and spiritually glorious, will be unveiled to your eyes. You are destined by Him, in this world and hereafter, to partake of their benefits, to share in their joys, and to obtain a portion of their sustaining grace. To each and every one of them you will, no doubt, attain.[27]

Notice that He says, "...in *this world* and hereafter...". This suggests to me that the door is open here and now, resonating with Maharishi's offer of enlightenment in this world. The message I get from both sides is we should take full advantage of our time in this physical life as the best preparation for our future in the worlds to come.

With all this in mind, let us turn once again to this quote from the *Bhagavad-Gita*: "Many births have passed for Me and for you also, O Arjuna. I know them all, but you know them not, O scorcher of enemies."[28] Since scripture often has multiple layers of meaning, could there be yet another way to understand this verse?

Viewing this passage as a whole, perhaps Krishna was not speaking of Himself and Arjuna as individuals, but rather as representing divinity and humanity, respectively. In that sense, Krishna would be aware and have memory of His previous manifestations. On the other hand, we humans do not have direct access to the memories of our ancestors or other people who have lived on this earth. This statement was given by Krishna to Arjuna in response to his question about how He gave this knowledge out at an earlier time. Krishna continues his answer by saying that He is unborn and imperishable, but that His birth in a physical body on this earth takes place from time to time. The context shows that it is Krishna's intention to educate Arjuna about His eternal divine nature, not to discuss reincarnation.

Of course, this is not the only way to interpret this passage. As with all scripture, each of us must be free to come to our own understanding. Personally, I find that adopting this point of view helps me to see how the *Bhagavad-Gita* is compatible with the Bahá'í teachings on the question of reincarnation.

Fear of God

In *Science of Being and Art of Living: Transcendental Meditation*, Maharishi says, "No fear of the name of God should have been instilled into the lives of people; no religions should have been based on the fear of God."[29] And yet, the Bahá'í writings contain many injunctions like this: "O people! Fear God, and disbelieve not in Him..."[30]

How can these two points of view be reconciled?

The way I see it, the fear of God comes in different forms, some healthy and some unhealthy. An unhealthy fear of God is born from ignorance of the true nature of God. Unscrupulous individuals prey on the uninformed, convincing them that God is cruel or vindictive, and they use the fear that they instill to gain some kind of power or control over people. This kind of fear causes people to turn away from God. In that same passage, Maharishi said, "And for the custodians of many strange religions, the word God is a magic word, used to control the understanding and religious destiny of many an innocent soul. God, the omnipresent essence of life, is presented as something to fear."[31]

A healthy fear of God, on the other hand, is born from understanding, and promotes the knowledge of God. The word "fear" in this sense is more like respect, awe, or even reverence. A more complete version of the quote of Bahá'u'lláh from above says this:

O people! Fear God, and disbelieve not in Him Whose grace hath surrounded all things, Whose mercy hath pervaded the contingent world, and the sovereign potency of Whose Cause hath encompassed both your inner and your outer beings, both your beginning and your end. Stand ye in awe of the Lord, and be of them that act uprightly.[32]

Here Bahá'u'lláh provides context for the injunction to fear God. He immediately talks about His grace, His mercy, and His sovereignty that encompasses our inner and outer being. This resonates with another reference from Maharishi, further in his passage: "that Being which dwells in the heart of everyone."[33]

Bahá'u'lláh then expands on the concept of "Fear God" by saying "Stand ye in awe of the Lord,..." and provides additional guidance on how to behave: "... and be of them that act uprightly."[34] The purpose of this healthy fear of God is to bring us closer to Him, rather than remaining heedless or unaware.

From another perspective, healthy fear can be seen as a normal human response to danger, and can be a strong motivating force. Fear of punishment plays a significant role in our social and spiritual development, perhaps more so in the early stages. Who among us has not hesitated to take part in some childhood mischief because we knew what would happen "when your father gets home"? As we grow up we learn that a wise parent is motivated by love, and punishes the child to guide him or her to right action. We would hope that as children develop a healthy fear of punishment, they also grow in love for their parents and eventually come to appreciate their wisdom in this matter. In the same way, may they grow in love for God.

A letter written on behalf of Shoghi Effendi says:

Only a relatively very highly evolved soul would always be disciplined by love alone. Fear of punishment, fear of the anger of God if we do evil, are needed to keep people's feet on the right path. Of course we should love God—but we must fear Him in the sense of a child fearing the righteous anger and chastisement of a parent; not cringe before Him as before a tyrant, but know His mercy exceeds His Justice![35]

The value of Maharishi's teaching is that it diminishes an unhealthy fear of God. Through the practice of TM, stress is reduced, ignorance is removed, and people begin to realize their true nature, which is to reflect the light of God. The experience of pure consciousness naturally restores a healthy relationship with that aspect of one's self.

This ability to eliminate fear calls to mind the following passage from the writings of Bahá'u'lláh:

In the treasuries of the knowledge of God there lieth concealed a knowledge which, when applied, will largely, though not wholly, eliminate fear. This knowledge, however, should be taught from childhood, as it will greatly aid in its elimination.[36]

As far as I know, the knowledge that Bahá'u'lláh refers to here has not been specifically or authoritatively identified by Himself, 'Abdu'l-Bahá, Shoghi Effendi, or any Bahá'í institution. We don't know exactly what that knowledge is, so we are free to come to our own understanding. For me, because the TM program has had such a beneficial effect on eliminating unhealthy fear from my heart, I believe that this could be one meaning of that passage. TM does not, in my experience, interfere with maintaining a healthy fear of God.

To sum up, then, it seems to me that it is up to us to decide whether we find conflict or compatibility between the teachings of Maharishi and the Bahá'í writings. These topics of suffering, reincarnation, and the fear of God have certainly challenged my thinking over the years. Rather than throwing up our hands in despair, we can instead persevere in our search for truth and get to the root of the question, so that potential conflict becomes a means to deepen our knowledge and faith.

Notes

1. Shoghi Effendi, *World Order of Bahá'u'lláh*, p 203

2. 'Abdu'l-Bahá, *Selections from the Writings of 'Abdu'l-Bahá*, p 132

3. 'Abdu'l-Bahá, *The Promulgation of Universal Peace*, p 51

4. Ibid, p 148

5. 'Abdu'l-Bahá, *Some Answered Questions*, p 233

6. 'Abdu'l-Bahá, *Paris Talks*, p 179

7. Ibid

8. Bahá'u'lláh, *The Hidden Words*, Persian #40

9. Bahá'u'lláh, *The Call of the Divine Beloved*, p 18

10. *Bhagavad-Gita - A New Translation and Commentary* 4:5

11. 'Abdu'l-Bahá, *Some Answered Questions*, p 130

12. *Bhagavad-Gita - A New Translation and Commentary* 2:18

13. 'Abdu'l-Bahá, *Paris Talks*, pp 90-91

14. *Bhagavad-Gita - A New Translation and Commentary* 2:18

15. 'Abdu'l-Bahá, *Paris Talks*, p 91

16. Maharishi Mahesh Yogi, *Bhagavad-Gita - A New Translation and Commentary*, p 73

17. *Bhagavad-Gita - A New Translation and Commentary* 2:27

18. Bahá'u'lláh, *The Call of the Divine Beloved*, p 44

19. *Bhagavad-Gita - A New Translation and Commentary* 2:22

20. Bahá'u'lláh, *Gleanings from the Writings of Bahá'u'lláh*, LXXXI

21. *Bhagavad-Gita - A New Translation and Commentary* 2:28

22. Bahá'u'lláh, *The Tabernacle of Unity*, p 49

23. *Bhagavad-Gita - A New Translation and Commentary* 6:45

24. Maharishi Mahesh Yogi, *Bhagavad-Gita - A New Translation and Commentary*, p 343

25. Ibid

26. 'Abdu'l-Bahá, *Some Answered Questions*, p 332

27. Bahá'u'lláh, *Gleanings from the Writings of Bahá'u'lláh*, CLIII

28. *Bhagavad-Gita - A New Translation and Commentary* 4:5

29. Maharishi Mahesh Yogi, *Science of Being and Art of Living: Transcendental Meditation*, p 306

30. Bahá'u'lláh, *The Summons of the Lord of Hosts*, p 40

31. Maharishi Mahesh Yogi, *Science of Being and Art of Living: Transcendental Meditation*, p 306

32. Bahá'u'lláh, *The Summons of the Lord of Hosts*, pp 40-41

33. Maharishi Mahesh Yogi, *Science of Being and Art of Living: Transcendental Meditation*, p 306

34. Bahá'u'lláh, *The Summons of the Lord of Hosts*, p 41

35. From a letter written on behalf of Shoghi Effendi to an individual believer, July 26, 1946, *Bahá'í Education*, compiled by the Research Department of the Universal House of Justice #133

36. Bahá'u'lláh, *Epistle to the Son of the Wolf*, p 32

Paths to God

The normal path to God in most parts of the world is through religious belief. People are taught from childhood about God and the Founder or Prophet of their religion. Each of these Holy Figures has a book where a divine message is recorded. After the Messenger departs this world, His followers have continued guidance. Those who believe, who follow the teachings in the book and observe the prescribed laws and rituals, trust that they will grow closer to God, both in this world and in the afterlife.

For some people, there is more to the story. Down through the ages there have always been a few seekers who may have followed the traditional path of belief, but also had what are often called mystical experiences. The mystic finds God through direct experience of divine love which he or she believes is reflected in the heart of every person.

Each of the major world religions has this mystical component. In Judaism, a group of people with this inclination were known as Kabbalists. In early Christianity, there were the Gnostics and others. Over the centuries several Christian monastic orders were founded, and more recently various charismatic movements have become popular. In Islam, there are various groups with names like Sufi and Dervish.

Sometimes relationships become difficult and strained between the more traditional followers of a religion on one side, versus the esoteric groups on the other. Those following the mystic path see their way as being a true connection to God, viewing those who attend mainstream churches and synagogues as being caught up in legal wrangling and meaningless rituals. For their part, the more traditional members of organized religions often view the mystics as foolish, useless, or even delusional.

The Bahá'í Faith encourages both approaches. Bahá'u'lláh wrote, "At one time We spoke in the language of the lawgiver; at another in that of the truth-seeker and the mystic..."[1] On the one hand there are practical rules and guidelines for how to live your life, how society can be organized, and how the Faith should be administered. There are institutions established by Bahá'u'lláh and upheld by 'Abdu'l-Bahá and Shoghi Effendi that should be respected and obeyed.

On the other hand, the Bahá'í Faith acknowledges the need for a mystical connection to God. The Universal House of Justice wrote, "For the core of religious faith is that mystic feeling that unites man with God. This state of spiritual communion can be brought about and maintained by means of meditation and prayer."[2]

Thus the mystical and the practical are two aspects of the same reality in Bahá'í life. The spiritual path is trodden with practical feet. Each Bahá'í is expected to develop both aspects in their activities and in their lives. Monasticism is forbidden, and yet prayer is obligatory. Prayer that leads to constructive action and service to humanity is encouraged.

In its own way, the TM program can also be seen as being both mystical and practical. The practicality of the technique itself, as well as the benefits it provides, have been discussed previously. As to the mystical aspect, rather than talking about meditation as a path to God, or about mystical experiences of divinity, Maharishi usually talks in terms of creative intelligence, Vedic Science, and the technology of the Unified Field. One of the big selling points of the TM program is that you don't have to believe in anything. You just do the technique, and it works. The goal is not God, per se, but the attainment of higher states of consciousness.

Some view that claim with skepticism. A group of Christians even took the matter to court, claiming that although TM is not promoted as a religion, it actually is, and thus should not be taught in public schools. A New Jersey court determined that "the SCI/TM course has a primary effect of advancing religion and religious concepts."[3] and thus did not permit it to be offered as a school course, in conformity with the principle of separation of church and state.

Whether TM is seen as a religion or not, I think most people will agree that Maharishi and the TM organization have made significant efforts to separate the TM program from religion. They use the language and concepts of science, publish research findings, and rarely talk about God or faith. The technique is offered as complementary to any religion, and followers and clergy from every creed and denomination practice TM. The success of the program has been fully documented, and is not based on belief. As long as you follow the instructions, no matter what you believe, it will work.

And yet many people find a systematic, mental approach to God to be too impersonal. They feel that a path of devotion to God is much more accessible if they have a personage of some kind that they can look to. For many people I knew at MIU, the path to enlightenment also had a personal, faith-based side. It seemed that devotion to Maharishi was a strong motivating factor for many, although he did not encourage it. Enlightenment was the goal, but that was abstract and far away. Some people confided in me that they did not have clear experiences of higher states of consciousness, and it was their faith in Maharishi that kept them there at MIU, on the program, whether as students or volunteer staff.

For the Bahá'ís and Christians I know who do not practice TM, the choice of paths is pretty clear. Most of them do not cultivate the experience of higher states of consciousness in any systematic way. The impersonal, experiential path of meditation is one that few choose to walk. Theirs is more, if not exclusively, the path of faith, of devotion. Meditation for them consists of thinking about passages from scripture and sacred writings after reading them, for inspiration and preparation for action. Communion with God is through prayer, which for some may provide an occasional experience of something beyond normal waking-state consciousness.

At the same time, their faith is not in a person, as such. They believe in a Personage, a Manifestation of God, like Jesus or Bahá'u'lláh. Recognizing Bahá'u'lláh as the Word of God, the Mouthpiece of God for this age gives Bahá'ís a direct connection to the words of God, which include practical guidance for daily living, as well as prayers for spiritual growth and personal transformation.

Whether these two paths, faith and experience, need to be treated independently is something that I have often pondered. Is a person naturally more inclined to one over the other? Is it our destiny? Why am I attracted to both of them? Can these paths overlap, or work side by side, or even join together at some point? Here are some ideas that have come to me over the years.

Two Aspects of Reality

Religious teachers and mystics often refer to two aspects of reality: visible and hidden. These may be said to be outer and inner, physical and spiritual, earthly and heavenly, or concrete and abstract realms of existence. These two aspects are sometimes considered in a hierarchical way, as with creation and Creator, or body and spirit. Although we are more aware of the tangible, from a spiritual point of view it is considered as less important, and ranks lower in a sense, than the intangible.

We also notice in nature two-sided, symmetrical relationships, reflections with subtle differences, as in right and left, or male and female. Some philosophers and thinkers have proposed that there could be a symmetrical relationship between the hidden and the visible, as in Plato's cave analogy. The people in the cave see shadows on the wall that reflect in mere silhouette the deeper reality of the object. The physical world can be seen to be an accurate representation of the spiritual, almost a mirror image, in some ways.

These two aspects of reality, with their symmetry and hierarchy, are beautifully portrayed in a Bahá'í symbol, known as the ring symbol, designed by 'Abdu'l-Bahá.

This symbol is composed of two Arabic/Persian letters, beh (ب, or B) and heh (ھ, or H), which are the two consonants in the word "Bahá". The beh is a horizontal line, gently curved upwards from the middle, and upturned to perpendicular at both ends. The heh is a bud-shaped oval that straddles both upturned ends of the beh. Right away you can see two examples of symmetry. The beh, with a heh at either end is symmetrical, and the heh itself, being split down the middle, is also symmetrical. So there is left-right symmetry.

The same shape is repeated below, an identical copy, in top-to-bottom symmetry.

The letter beh gets repeated in between, dividing those two. And it is also turned on its side, joining them. And finally, there are two stars, arranged symmetrically on the left and right.

'Abdu'l-Bahá explains that there are three levels to the symbol, overall. The top level represents the world of God, and the bottom level represents the world of creation. They are both the same, yet separate, one reflecting the other. Between them, the plain beh symbol with no heh, represents the realm of the Manifestation of God, the Founder of each of the major world religions, such as Jesus, Bahá'u'lláh, or Krishna. This Manifestation of God is between us and God, and also, like the beh symbol turned on its side, joins humanity to God. Also at that middle level, each five-pointed star is said to represent a human (head, arms, and legs). Those two stars represent the Báb and Bahá'u'lláh, the physical, twin Manifestations of God for the Bahá'í dispensation—the time we are living in now.

What interests me in this symbol is there are both top-to-bottom and left-to-right symmetries. Most obvious is the top-to-bottom symmetry between the world of God and the world of creation. And yet there is also a left-to-right symmetry within the world of God. And that gets mirrored in a similar left-to-right symmetry in the world of creation. Could these two left-to-right symmetries in the world of God and the world of creation correspond to each other in some way? Are there possibly two aspects of reality in the world of creation that somehow mirror two aspects of reality in the world of God? I have not found any commentary in the Bahá'í writings specifically on this idea, but the possibility intrigues me. In fact, it suggests to me a way to resolve the question of how the path of belief and the path of mystical experience may be related to one another. Maybe there is a geometry of relationships in the shape of a pentangle, a five-pointed star.

Star Geometry

Here is one way I like to think about our path (or paths) to God. To start with, the Bahá'í teachings say that God, in His Essence is unknowable:

> To every discerning and illumined heart it is evident that God, the unknowable Essence, the divine Being, is immensely exalted beyond every human attribute, such as corporeal existence, ascent and descent, egress and regress. Far be it from His glory that human tongue should adequately recount His praise, or that human heart comprehend His fathomless mystery. He is and hath ever been veiled in the ancient eternity of His Essence, and will remain in His Reality everlastingly hidden from the sight of men.[4]

But we can know God through His Manifestations, like Jesus, Krishna, or Bahá'u'lláh. He continues:

> The door of the knowledge of the Ancient of Days being thus closed in the face of all beings, the Source of infinite grace... hath caused those luminous Gems of Holiness to appear out of the realm of the spirit, in the noble form of the human temple, and be made manifest unto all men, that they may impart unto the world the mysteries of the unchangeable Being, and tell of the subtleties of His imperishable Essence. These sanctified Mirrors, these Dayspring of ancient glory are one and all the Exponents on earth of Him Who is the central Orb of the universe, its Essence and ultimate Purpose. From Him proceed their knowledge and power; from Him is derived their sovereignty.[5]

This is perhaps the first instance of a hidden/visible relationship, where the Essence of God is completely unattainable, absolutely hidden, while the Manifestation of God by comparison is in some way visible and attainable. Clearly this would be a hierarchical, top-to-bottom, relationship.

And what do we know about the Manifestation of God? Often the Bahá'í writings talk about this concept in terms of the Will of God.

> The essence of belief in Divine unity consisteth in regarding Him Who is the Manifestation of God and Him

Who is the invisible, the inaccessible, the unknowable Essence as one and the same. By this is meant that whatever pertaineth to the former, all His acts and doings, whatever He ordaineth or forbiddeth, should be considered, in all their aspects, and under all circumstances, and without any reservation, as identical with the Will of God Himself.[6]

The Bahá'í writings also refer to the Manifestation of God as the Word of God.

Know that, while the Manifestations of God possess infinite virtues and perfections, They occupy only three stations... The third station is that of divine manifestation and heavenly splendour, which is the Word of God, the everlasting Grace, and the Holy Spirit. ...Now, the reality of prophethood, which is the Word of God and the state of perfect divine manifestation, has neither beginning nor end... [7]

Both the Will of God and the Word of God seem to be in some sense primal realities of the Manifestation of God. Although these are abstract concepts, maybe we can think of them as two aspects of the Manifestation, one more concealed, the other more revealed, in a relative sense. For example, a person's will is invisible and cannot be directly perceived, yet a word is spoken and heard. So, while both Will and Word are intangible aspects of the Manifestation of God, maybe we can think of them as existing in a left-right symmetry, in which the left side is hidden and the right side is in a sense, more visible. Thus we have now three ideas, the completely inaccessible, unknowable Essence of God, and the two aspects of His Manifestation: Will and Word, one more hidden, the other relatively more manifest. Suppose we arrange them into a triangle like this:

So we identify a hierarchical relationship between the Essence of God to the Manifestation, and for the Manifestation we suggest a left-right relationship, perhaps a symmetry in some way, between Will and Word.

At the level of Will and Word, two corresponding aspects of reality come to mind. Related to Will is nature. Bahá'u'lláh said, "Nature is God's Will and is its expression in and through the contingent world."[8] We may thus want to place nature at the same level as Will, but farther from the center. On the other hand, there seems to be a close relationship between the Word and its expression in revelation, such as in this quote from Bahá'u'lláh: "...a Word shining above the horizon of the Will of the All-Glorious in this Revelation..."[9] In this way, we might expand our diagram like this:

```
                    Unknowable
                     Essence

                        /\
                       /  \
                      /    \
    Nature      Will      Word      Revelation
```

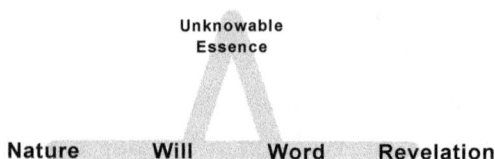

This illustrates the two aspects of divine Manifestation, Will and Word, and how they correspond, in an abstract way to nature and revelation. At a more expressed level, yet still within the level of the Manifestation of God, we might place the Creator, an agent that corresponds to the hidden, impersonal force of nature. At that same level, the concept of Prophet as the visible, individualized, personal agent of revelation. These two aspects of the Manifestation, although still abstract, give us the feeling of an actor performing actions, which brings us closer to our level of reality.

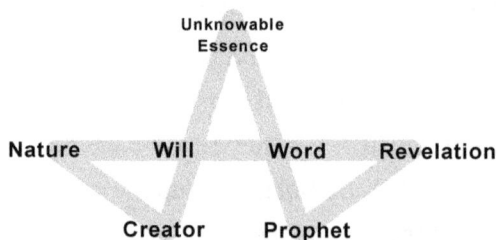

```
                    Unknowable
                     Essence

                        /\
                       /  \
    Nature      Will      Word      Revelation
                      \    /
                       \  /
                    Creator   Prophet
```

This concept of impersonal and personal aspects of the Manifestation of God correspond, I believe, quite well to Maharishi's explanation of the impersonal and personal aspects of God. For example, describing the impersonal aspect of God, he says, "It is the creator, maintainer, and sustainer of the world. It is called the creator because It is the basis of all creation; all creation comes out of It."[10] Describing the personal aspect of God, Maharishi says, "The personal aspect of God necessarily has form, qualities, and features, likes and dislikes, and the ability to command the entire existence of the cosmos, the process of evolution, and all that there is in creation."[11]

The next point, where the lines from the two sides join together, I see as the point of unity. There is the deep unity between the two aspects of the Manifestation. And there is also unity between the Manifestation and humanity. This point, we can suggest, corresponds to the human reality of the Manifestation of God.

Unknowable
Essence

Nature   Will   Word   Revelation

Creator   Prophet

Unity

The point of unity can also be the point of unity for humanity in general, and for each of us as individuals. It is the point where we can know God, through His Manifestation. Bahá'u'lláh says: "O Son of Being! Thy heart is My home; sanctify it for My descent."[12] For us, this point of unity can be said to be our sanctified heart. Maharishi says, "The impersonal God is that Being which dwells in the heart of everyone."[13]

Bahá'u'lláh continues, "Thy spirit is My place of revelation; cleanse it for My manifestation."[14] These words point to a lofty station for us, as well as the means to achieve it. It doesn't come automatically. We have to do something for it. We need to walk a spiritual path, of some kind, to move from where we are to where we want to be.

I see two paths that we can follow to reach to this point of unity: belief and experience. And this symmetrical geometry helps me understand how they are different, yet similar.

Unknowable
Essence

Nature   Will   Word   Revelation

Creator   Prophet

Unity

Belief   Experience

To me, belief springs from the hidden side of our reality. It is intuitive. You cannot put your finger on it. It's just there. But it is nurtured by something visible, something tangible. You believe in the words of a Prophet, of a religious teacher. You have scripture to guide you to His Revelation, with divinely revealed laws. Following them, you put your faith into action, and it is strengthened. In this way you move closer to that point of Unity, which is the Manifestation of God on earth.

On the other hand, I see meditation as starting from the outer, visible aspect of reality, and moving towards the inner, hidden side. In TM, for example, no belief is necessary. You simply use a sound, a mantra, to experience finer and finer levels of thought until you transcend thought altogether and experience the source of thought, the Unified Field of Natural Law. As that experience grows, due to the mind-body connection, profound physiological changes take place in your nervous system. Your mind and actions become purified, and you find yourself living more and more in tune with natural law. Since nature is God's Will, following the path of experience of higher states of consciousness should ultimately lead to Unity with the divine, the experience known as Brahman Consciousness.

To sum up, our hidden, intuitive side where belief and faith reside is nourished by the visible, personal aspect of God's Manifestation—His Prophet and Revelation—by intoning His prayers and meditating on the revealed Word. In the other direction, the more overt, rational side of our mind can access the hidden, impersonal aspect of God's Manifestation—the Creator and Unified Field of Natural Law—through meditation techniques such as TM that allow the mind to transcend thought and directly experience pure consciousness. These two paths become one at the point of unity, the human heart.

Finding the Lord as God

Divinity is expressed in the *Bhagavad-Gita*, the scripture of the Vedas, as a Manifestation of God, Lord Krishna. He says, "Established in Unity, he who worships Me abiding in all beings, in whatever way he lives, that yogi lives in Me."[15]

In his commentary on that particular verse, Maharishi says, "To live through the various phases of man's life on earth while abiding in the worship of God, is the character of a particular level of consciousness."[16] Here Maharishi clearly identifies worship of Krishna ("worships Me") as "worship of God". This conforms well with Bahá'u'lláh's teaching that we worship God through His Manifestation. Bahá'u'lláh wrote: "The essence of belief in Divine unity consisteth in regarding Him Who is the Manifestation of God and Him Who is the invisible, the inaccessible, the unknowable Essence as one and the same."[17]

Maharishi first published his commentary on the *Bhagavad-Gita* in 1967. In the early days of the TM organization, there was more mention of God and spirituality. For example, it was most widely known as the Spiritual Regeneration Movement for about a decade. But by the 1970's it was being referred to as the International Foundation for the Science of Creative Intelligence. That's how it was introduced to me, and it made sense. They used words like "science" (the Science of Creative Intelligence), "technology" (the technology of the Unified Field), and "technique" (the TM technique). As I understand it, Maharishi adopted this language to appeal to the Western mindset, to reach people of every religion and of no religion.

Taking this perspective can only go so far, as the plaintiffs in the New Jersey court case pointed out. Eventually, when you are talking about pure consciousness, an Absolute, and creative intelligence, people start thinking about God and religion. It certainly seems to be a path to God, in some way. But at the same time, keeping the focus on science, verifiable measurement, and published articles in highly-respected academic journals tends to remove much of the fear and superstition that has grown up around "mysticism" over the centuries. In this way, and because Maharishi has in the past talked about TM as a way to God-consciousness, I feel confident in considering it a technique that can bring you closer to God, but which does not require belief in God.

The question now becomes: Is TM all you need? Does this technique that cultivates higher states of consciousness bring you all the way to God? Certain passages from Maharishi's commentary on the *Bhagavad-Gita* suggest that it does. For example, he says:

The state of consciousness that knows the glory of the great Lord of all beings is divine. It is developed through constant and regular practice of meditation and the experience of transcendental Being, which eventually

179

brings cosmic consciousness, the state in which the heart and mind are fully matured. This full development of the capacities of heart and mind enables a man to understand and live the divine Being.[18]

So there you have it. No religion is necessary. Or is that what it really means? It certainly speaks to the value of meditation in finding our way to God, the "great Lord." What does Bahá'u'lláh have to say on this topic? It seems there may be harmony at a deep level, when you look carefully. This harmony is suggested in the first passage in the Book of Certitude, where Bahá'u'lláh says:

No man shall attain the shores of the ocean of true understanding except he be detached from all that is in heaven and on earth. Sanctify your souls, O ye peoples of the world, that haply ye may attain that station which God hath destined for you ...[19]

Here we find encouragement to purify our consciousness from everything pertaining to the world, to cleanse our souls of all earthly desires and of human knowledge, with the goal of attaining a high station that is our true destiny. What is that station, according to Bahá'u'lláh? That station is the recognition of the Manifestation of God. That is our first duty. In the Most Holy Book, Bahá'u'lláh wrote:

The first duty prescribed by God for His servants is the recognition of Him Who is the Dayspring of His

Revelation and the Fountain of His laws, Who repre-
senteth the Godhead in both the Kingdom of His Cause
and the world of creation.[20]

How does this recognition take place? Looking again at
our star geometry, with belief and experience as two kinds of
paths, both might lead to recognition of the Manifestation of
God. I see our movement on either of these two paths as part
of a flow. The flow comes from God and returns to Him. It is a
flow of love and of knowledge.

It is a flow of love through the Creator, as Bahá'u'lláh said:
"O Son of Man! I loved thy creation, hence I created thee.
Wherefore, do thou love Me, that I may name thy name and fill
thy soul with the spirit of life."[21] The path of experience, then,
should lead to God.

It is also a flow of knowledge, through the revealed Word
of God, as in these words of Bahá'u'lláh: "Sow the seeds of
My divine wisdom in the pure soil of thy heart, and water
them with the water of certitude, that the hyacinths of My
knowledge and wisdom may spring up fresh and green in the
sacred city of thy heart."[22] The path of belief, then, should also
lead to God.

As our belief and knowledge increase, as our experience
and love flow, we recognize ever more clearly God's Manifestation—be it Jesus, Krishna, or Bahá'u'lláh. This is how
we know God, as this recognition occurs in the heart of the
sanctified soul.

At the beginning of this book, I said that as far back as I could remember, as far back as I knew, God was there. In my life I have learned that as we purify our nervous systems through direct experience of the pure field of creative intelligence, and as we strengthen our faith through devotion, service, and immersion in the revealed Word of God, we begin to recognize more and more not only that God is there, but also that God is here—here in our hearts.

Bahá'u'lláh teaches that we know God through His Manifestation. He said, "He Who is everlastingly hidden from the eyes of men can never be known except through His Manifestation..."[23]

Upon first reading those words, my meditating self was inspired: "We can know God."

My Bahá'í self noticed "...through His Manifestation."

"But we can *know God!*" exclaimed my meditating self.

"Yes, but *through His Manifestation.*" cautioned my Bahá'í self.

For a long time I wondered if there might be a conflict, and my heart was not truly at peace. I couldn't be certain. But over time, as stresses dissolved from mind and heart, both sides opened up, and started listening and looking deeper. The clouds of doubt and confusion parted, and the sun began to shine through.

O My brother! A pure heart is as a mirror; cleanse it with the burnish of love and severance from all save God, that the true sun may shine therein and the eternal morning dawn. Then wilt thou clearly see the meaning of 'Earth and heaven cannot contain Me; what can alone contain Me is the heart of him that believeth in Me.' And thou wilt take up thy life in thy hand and with infinite longing cast it before thy newly found Beloved.[24] - Bahá'u'lláh

Notes

1. Bahá'u'lláh, *Epistle to the Son of the Wolf*, p 15

2. The Universal House of Justice, *Prayer and Devotional Life* #71

3. *Malnak v. Yogi*, Opinion of the Court #10

4. Bahá'u'lláh, *Kitáb-i-Íqán (The Book of Certitude)*, p 98

5. Ibid, pp 99-100

6. Bahá'u'lláh, *Gleanings from the Writings of Bahá'u'lláh*, LXXXIV

7. 'Abdu'l-Bahá, *Some Answered Questions*, pp 172,173

8. Bahá'u'lláh, *Tablets of Bahá'u'lláh*, p 142

9. Bahá'u'lláh, *The Summons of the Lord of Hosts*, p 19

10. Maharishi Mahesh Yogi, *Science of Being and Art of Living: Transcendental Meditation*, p 302

11. Ibid, p 306

12. Bahá'u'lláh, *The Hidden Words*, Arabic #59

13. Maharishi Mahesh Yogi, *Science of Being and Art of Living: Transcendental Meditation*, p 306

14. Bahá'u'lláh, *The Hidden Words*, Arabic #59

15. *Bhagavad-Gita - A New Translation and Commentary* 6:31

16. Maharishi Mahesh Yogi, *Bhagavad-Gita - A New Translation and Commentary*, p 329

17. Bahá'u'lláh, *Gleanings from the Writings of Bahá'u'lláh*, LXXXIV

18. Maharishi Mahesh Yogi, *Bhagavad-Gita - A New Translation and Commentary*, p 328

19. Bahá'u'lláh, *Kitáb-i-Íqán (The Book of Certitude)*, p 3

20. Bahá'u'lláh, *Kitáb-i-Aqdas (The Most Holy Book)*, p 19

21. Bahá'u'lláh, *The Hidden Words*, Arabic #4

22. Ibid, Persian #33

23. Bahá'u'lláh, *Gleanings from the Writings of Bahá'u'lláh*, XX

24. Bahá'u'lláh, *The Call of the Divine Beloved*, p 31

Afterword

In one of the Narnia books, *Prince Caspian*, the four children are pulled into Narnia at a time of great need. Prince Caspian, the talking animals, dwarves, and other mythical creatures are being threatened by an evil king. They have blown a horn that brought the children to this magical land, and which may also summon Aslan, the awe-inspiring lion that represents the Divine Presence in that world.

The children arrive, confused at first, but gradually realize that they are in Narnia. They are met by a dwarf, and together they must find their way to the meeting place of the other creatures preparing to fight the evil king. As they hike through the woods, trying to avoid enemy forces, Lucy, the youngest, sees Aslan up on a ridge. She excitedly tells the other children, but they don't see him. She says they must all follow Aslan, but she is outvoted. They continue on their way, only to be blocked by the king's soldiers, and have to retreat back the way they came, wasting a full day of precious time.

That night Lucy wakes up out of a deep sleep and is attracted through the trees to discover Aslan standing there, waiting for her. She rushes to him, buries her head in his mane, grateful for this long-awaited reunion, and happy that now all of the problems will be solved. Aslan asks her why she didn't follow him earlier that day. She said she could not, because the others did not. He helps her realize that she actually could have followed him.

Now they must move quickly. Aslan tells Lucy to go, wake up her siblings and the dwarf, and tell them that he is here. They won't be able to see him at first, he says, but they might later on. In despair, Lucy cries that she cannot do this. They won't believe her. She buries her head in Aslan's mane, and discovers that she has gained a small measure of courage.

"'Now child,' said Aslan, when they had left the trees behind them. 'I will wait here. Go and wake the others and tell them to follow. If they will not, then you at least must follow me alone.'"[1]

Writing this book to discuss possible connections between the return of Christ, the Bahá'í Revelation, and Maharishi's revival of the Vedas is not the end of the story for me. It is just a beginning. I expect to continue exploring these and other, related topics for some time to come. Will you?

"The Hand of Divine bounty proffereth unto you the Water of Life. Hasten and drink your fill." - Bahá'u'lláh[2]

Notes

1. C.S. Lewis, *Prince Caspian*, p 126
2. Bahá'u'lláh, *Gleanings from the Writings of Bahá'u'lláh*, CVI

References

'Abdu'l-Bahá. *Paris Talks*. London, Bahá'í Publishing Trust, 1972.

———. *The Promulgation of Universal Peace*. Wilmette, Bahá'í Publishing Trust, 1982.

———. *Selections from the Writings of 'Abdu'l-Bahá*. Bahá'í World Centre, 1978.

———. *Some Answered Questions*. Bahá'í World Centre, 2014.

Bahá'í Prayers. Wilmette, Bahá'í Publishing Trust, 1982.

Bahá'u'lláh. *The Call of the Divine Beloved*. Bahá'í World Centre, 2018.

———. *Epistle to the Son of the Wolf*. Wilmette, Bahá'í Publishing Trust, 1979.

———. *Gleanings from the Writings of Bahá'u'lláh*. Wilmette, Bahá'í Publishing Trust, 1976.

———. *The Hidden Words*. Wilmette, Bahá'í Publishing Trust, 1975.

———. *Kitáb-i-Aqdas (The Most Holy Book)*. Bahá'í World Centre, 1992.

———. *Kitáb-i-Íqán (The Book of Certitude)*. Wilmette, Bahá'í Publishing Trust, 1974.

———. *Prayers and Meditations*. Wilmette, Bahá'í Publishing Trust, 1979.

————. *The Summons of the Lord of Hosts*. Bahá'í World Centre, 2002.

————. *The Tabernacle of Unity*. Bahá'í World Centre, 2006.

————. *Tablets of Bahá'u'lláh*. Bahá'í World Centre, 1978.

Barbour, Ian G. *When Science Meets Religion*, HarperCollins, 2000.

The Bible. Revised Standard Version, Oxford UP, 1962.

Carus, Paul. *The Gospel Of Buddha*. Chicago And London, The Open Court Publishing Company, 1915.

Dillbeck, Susan, and Michael Dillbeck. "The Maharishi Technology of the Unified Field in Education: Principles, Practice, and Research." Maharishi European Research University. www.meru-vlodrop.nl/ wp-content/uploads/2012/10/ UF-education-Dillbeck.pdf, 2021

Effendi, Shoghi. *Bahá'í Education*. Compiled by the Research Department of the Universal House of Justice, Bahá'í World Centre 1976.

————. *God Passes By*. Wilmette, Bahá'í Publishing Trust, 1974.

————. *The World Order of Bahá'u'lláh*. Wilmette, Bahá'í Publishing Trust, 1980.

Goldberg, Philip. *The TM Program: The Way to Fulfillment: The Transcendental Meditation Program Is a Proven Approach to Developing the Full Human Potential: What it Is, How it Works, What it Does*. New York, Holt, Rinehart and Winston, 1976.

The Hymnal. Presbyterian Board of Christian Education, 1945.

The Koran. Translated by J.M. Rodwell, London, J.M. Dent, 1909.

Lewis, C.S. *The Lion, the Witch and the Wardrobe.* HarperCollins Children's Books 1950.

———. *Prince Caspian.* HarperCollins Children's Books 1951.

Maharishi Mahesh Yogi. *Bhagavad-Gita - A New Translation and Commentary.* MIU Press, 1976.

———. *Science of Being and Art of Living: Transcendental Meditation.* Vlodrop, Maharishi Vedic University Press, 2019.

———. "Celebrating 12 January 2008." *Global Good News.* globalgoodnews.com.

Malnak v. Yogi 440 F. Supp. 1284. D.N.J., 1977.

Prayer and Devotional Life. Wilmette, Bahá'í Publishing, 2019.

Wilson, H. H. *Rig Veda (translation and commentary)* www.wisdomlib.org/ hinduism/book/rig--veda-english-translation.

Permissions

Excerpts from the writings of Bahá'u'lláh, 'Abdu'l-Bahá, and Shoghi Effendi used with permission.

Excerpts from *The TM Program: The Way to Fulfillment: The Transcendental Meditation Program Is a Proven Approach to Developing the Full Human Potential: What it Is, How it Works, What it Does* used with permission.

Excerpts from *Revised Standard Version of the Bible*, copyright © 1946, 1952, and 1971 National Council of the Churches of Christ in the United States of America used by permission. All rights reserved.

Excerpts from *The Lion, the Witch and the Wardrobe* by CS Lewis © copyright 1950 CS Lewis Pte Ltd, and *Prince Caspian* by CS Lewis © copyright 1951 CS Lewis Pte Ltd used with permission.

Excerpts from *Bhagavad-Gita - A New Translation and Commentary, Science of Being and Art of Living: Transcendental Meditation*, by Maharishi Mahesh Yogi, and "The Maharishi Technology of the Unified Field in Education: Principles, Practice, and Research" used with permission.

All other quotes are in the public domain or considered fair use.

Acknowledgements

I wish to thank May Abhar, Bill McIlvride, Felicity Rawlings-Sanaei, Sandra Briand, Sue Brown, and Wadi Bounouar for reviewing drafts of the text and offering valuable suggestions. I am also grateful to members of the Bahá'í community of Fairfield, Iowa who from 1981 through 1988 helped shape some of the ideas in this book through thoughtful conversation. Finally, a special shout out to Ava Abhar for the cover stars.

www.ingramcontent.com/pod-product-compliance
Lightning Source LLC
LaVergne TN
LVHW041216080426
835508LV00011B/974